Sunset

Oriental
COOK BOOK

By the Editors of Sunset Books
and Sunset Magazine

Lane Publishing Co. · Menlo Park, California

Coordinating Editor
Cornelia Fogle

Research & Text
Elizabeth Friedman

Special Consultant
Linda Anusasananan
Associate Editor,
Sunset Magazine

Design
Lea Damiano Phelps

Illustrations
Jacqueline Osborn

Photography
Nikolay Zurek

Photo Editor
Lynne B. Morrall

Editor, Sunset Books: David E. Clark

First printing April 1984

Beijing to Bangkok...

The mysterious lands of the Far East feature some of the world's most exotic, intriguing, and exciting cuisines—cuisines that have, in recent years, gained popularity with Westerners open to experimenting with new dishes and flavors. We invite you to explore with us the fascinating cookery of this region, with its emphasis on fresh ingredients, bold seasonings, and attractive presentation.

In these recipes you'll discover creative combinations of colors, flavors, and textures that will add a lively, fresh dimension to your menus. We've collected a delicious sampling from China, Japan, Korea, and nine nations of Southeast Asia. Many of the ingredients and cooking methods may already be familiar to you; some probably will not be. Among the well-known favorites are won ton soup and crisp tempura, delicate sushi and spicy curries. And among the many dishes likely to be new to you are miso soup, tea-smoked duck, and Singapore satay.

Our special thanks to Kiyoko Ishimoto, Dorothy Louie, and the Department of Asian Languages at Stanford University for their assistance; and to Cynthia Scheer for her help with photography. Our thanks, also, to Rebecca La Brum for a thorough, yet sensitive, editing of the manuscript.

For their generosity in sharing props for use in photographs, our appreciation goes to The Abacus, Brass International, House of Today, Kuromatsu Oriental Art, William Ober Co., and Williams-Sonoma Kitchenware.

Cover: Sharing the spotlight is a quartet from the cuisines of the Orient, identified clockwise from top left. From Korea come Barbecued Short Ribs (page 69), shown with *kim chee* and carrot flowers. Assorted *sushi* is a highlight from Japan—Rolled Sushi (page 43) and Hand-shaped Sushi (page 44) are presented with wasabi paste and a delicate radish fan. Representing Southeast Asia is Singapore Satay with Pressed Rice Cubes (page 86), accompanied by Peanut Sauce (page 92) for dipping, and a refreshing garnish of Marinated Cucumbers (page 96) from Thailand. Colorful finger food from China includes Fried Won Ton (page 16) with hot mustard and catsup, Marinated Lotus Root (page 36), and crisp snow peas. Photograph by Nikolay Zurek. Cover design by Naganuma Design & Direction and Lynne B. Morrall.

米 Contents

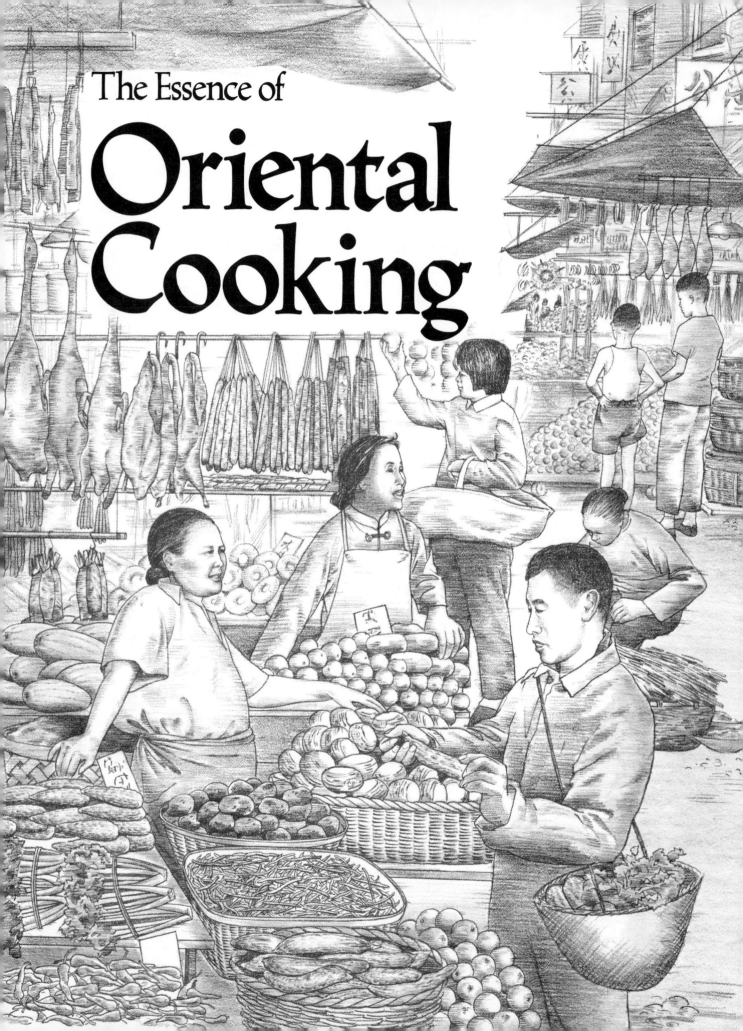

The Essence of Oriental Cooking

A Region of Shared Traditions

More and more, it seems, the way we eat echoes long-standing traditions from the Orient. We're eating less meat and more fish; we like our vegetables crisp and our sauces light.

In this context, Oriental cooking seems less mysterious and begins to make good common sense. It's a style that stresses freshness and natural flavors; it's economical, in terms of both time and ingredients. Rapid stir-fries from China, simple soups from Thailand, donburi from Japan—many dishes can be ready for the table in a matter of minutes. And no cooks the world over are better than Asians at stretching just a bit of meat to feed many.

The variety of cooking styles from this part of the world is almost limitless. From the succulent stir-fries of Canton to Japan's delicate sushi, from the rich, spicy curries of Southeast Asia to Korea's rib-sticking barbecue, there is literally something for everyone to enjoy. Now, more than ever, is the time to explore the cooking of the Orient.

Over the centuries, Asian countries have freely exchanged culinary styles and practices, as well as adopting ingredients and cooking techniques from European explorers and traders. It's not surprising, then, that the similarities among Oriental cuisines are so striking. Most notable is a common thread of shared ingredients and similar (if not quite identical) cooking methods. Pervasive, too, is a deeply rooted attitude of appreciation and respect for both ingredients and the dishes made from them.

Some Common Staples

Throughout Asia, rice is truly the staff of life. Typically served as a side dish in Western cultures, it is at the very heart of Oriental meals: it's the primary offering, providing the neutral base upon which the myriad flavors of other dishes can build. First cultivated in Asia, it's the chief source of nourishment throughout most of the region.

Three types of rice are used in Asia. The long-grain rice familiar to Westerners is favored in China and in much of Southeast Asia; in Japan, Korea, and the Philippines, short or medium-grain rice is preferred. Sticky rice—sticky-textured and slightly sweet—is first choice in Laos and northern Thailand.

Though rice is often served plain and unseasoned, this is by no means the only way it's prepared. It also forms the base for any number of special dishes—among them China's fried rice, Japan's sushi, Malaysia's aromatic spiced rice, and the spectacular yellow rice cone of Indonesia.

Because rice is so important in Oriental cooking, we've chosen to illustrate headings throughout this book with the character (Chinese/Japanese, Korean, or Thai) meaning "rice." The symbol is the same in Chinese and Japanese (left); the Korean (center) and Thai (right) characters are quite different.

米　쌀　ข้าว

Another important staple is the versatile soybean, basic ingredient for a variety of products. (Even the crisp sprouts are used, contributing crunchy texture to stir-fries and other dishes.) One of the most important soy derivatives is bean curd. Called "meat without bones" in China, this high-protein food is a favorite with Oriental cooks. Some Japanese res-

Shoppers choose dinner ingredients from baskets heaped with market produce; ducks and sausages hang from bamboo rods.

taurants serve nothing but bean curd dishes; in Southeast Asia, you'll find it stuffed, stir-fried, and simmered in soups.

Soy sauce, made from fermented soybeans, is just as essential to Oriental cooking as salt is to Western cuisines. This dark seasoning sauce adds savory, salty, and sometimes slightly sweet flavor to dishes all over Asia. Certain other soy products play important roles in just one or a few countries; Indonesia's tempeh (a dense-textured, cheeselike food made from fermented soybeans) and Japan's miso are two examples.

As you leaf through this book, you'll note that favorite seasonings do vary from one country to another—but you'll also find that some flavorings are popular everywhere. Garlic, ginger, chiles, and fresh coriander flavor dishes from Beijing to Bangkok.

Cooking Techniques

Many of the cooking methods used in the Orient— steaming, braising, and deep-frying, for example— are familiar to Western cooks. Stir-frying may be new to you, though. This Chinese technique is also important in the cooking of Korea and Southeast Asia; you'll find the process explained and illustrated on page 26.

When you stir-fry, don't rely exclusively on the cooking times given in individual recipes—depending on the intensity of the heat source you use and on the thickness of food slices, times can vary greatly. Take the time to familiarize yourself with the overall sequence of events in stir-frying, and use our cooking times only as a guide. Keep in mind, too, that it's essential to have everything prepared before you begin to stir-fry. Once the wok is hot, there's no time for slicing or dicing.

You won't find a wok in a Japanese kitchen, for Japan is one Asian country whose cuisine doesn't require a mastery of stir-frying. As a rule, the Japanese prefer the delicate and pure flavors of foods cooked in water (or by steam heat) to the taste of those cooked in oil. Popular deep-fried dishes such as tempura are relatively recent additions, absorbed into Japanese cooking from foreign cuisines.

A History of Reverence for Food

For reasons ranging from terrain to religious restrictions to simple scarcity, Asian cooks have always had to make do with less. As a result, they place a special value on their food, more so than cooks in

cultures where the food supply has always been plentiful.

In Japan, limited choice and availability of ingredients have shaped a cuisine famed for its elegance, simplicity, and painstaking presentation. Since Buddhist dietary law for centuries forbade the killing of four-footed animals, the Japanese turned to the sea, making creative use of fish, shellfish, and seaweed. And because much of their country's terrain does not permit farming, they learned how to exploit fully any and all cultivable land. Rice, the nation's staple grain, and space-efficient root vegetables play an important role in Japanese cooking.

In response to their dietary limitations, the Japanese applied a simple principle: make more of less. They learned to delight in the overall appearance of a dish—in the colors, shapes, and textures of the food, and in its presentation on elegant serving pieces. An appreciation of the different seasons and the foods associated with them is also an integral part of Japanese dining. The first strawberries of spring, even if there are only one or two to enjoy, are prized for their beauty and sweet succulence. Symbolism is often apparent in a traditional Japanese meal; for instance, a carrot slice may be carved into a maple leaf in honor of autumn's changing colors. A Japanese meal, then, does not simply satisfy basic needs. It is a feast for the eyes and for the soul as well.

The cooking of China, like that of Japan, has been influenced by the necessity of making do with less. Confronted with frequent famine, a large population, a limited supply of fuel, and a relatively small area of arable land, the Chinese adapted with style. They developed fuel-efficient methods of cooking (stir-frying is the best example of this) and overlooked nothing as a potential food source. Foraging in the forest brought forth black fungus; from the ocean came the strange-looking sea cucumber (a well-fed Westerner would probably dismiss both items as inedible). The Chinese learned to treat every food with respect. And they learned how to make anything edible taste good: even the most meager offerings were worthy of careful seasoning and saucing.

For China's royalty and leisure class, dining well was an important part of the upper-class lifestyle. The chefs of the great dynasties were constantly challenged to create elaborate dishes with harmonious, exciting combinations of flavors, textures, and colors. This tradition of creativity has been carried on by chefs for centuries, helping to form a cuisine balanced by opposing influences— scarcity and abundance, tradition and innovation— but always and above all, centered on a love of and respect for good food.

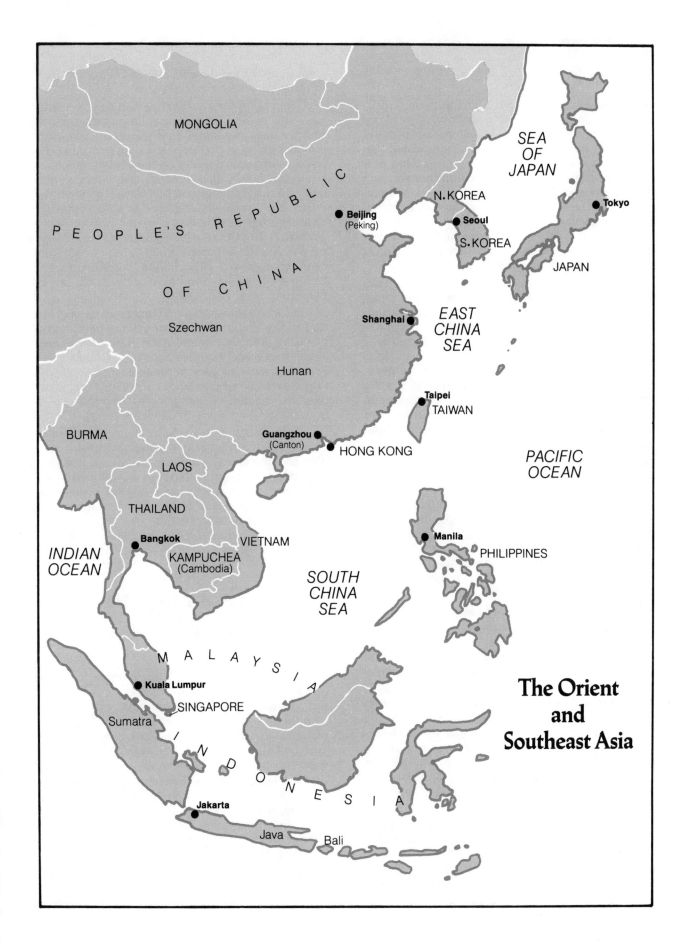

MONGOLIA

PEOPLE'S REPUBLIC

OF CHINA

SEA
OF
JAPAN

N. KOREA

● Beijing
(Peking)

● Seoul

S. KOREA

● Tokyo

JAPAN

Szechwan

Hunan

● Shanghai

EAST
CHINA
SEA

BURMA

● Taipei
TAIWAN

Guangzhou ●
(Canton)

● HONG KONG

PACIFIC
OCEAN

LAOS

THAILAND

● Bangkok

VIETNAM

KAMPUCHEA
(Cambodia)

INDIAN
OCEAN

SOUTH
CHINA
SEA

● Manila

PHILIPPINES

M A L A Y S I A

● Kuala Lumpur

SINGAPORE

Sumatra

I N D O N E S I A

● Jakarta

Java

Bali

**The Orient
and
Southeast Asia**

Foreign Influences

Some sources claim that Italy's famous pasta is really an adaptation of Chinese *mein*—discovered by Marco Polo during his adventures in China, then brought back to his homeland. Others have speculated that sauerkraut was inspired by Oriental pickled cabbage. The extent of the culinary connections among the countries of Asia, and among these lands and the rest of the world, is nothing short of astonishing. Immigration, colonization, trade, and invasion have produced a blend of native and foreign elements that makes these cuisines some of the most complex and intriguing in the world.

Chinese influences are apparent all over Asia. The charcoal-fired hot pot common in both Japan and Korea was first used in China, as was the round-bottomed wok (found with slight differences in Korea and Southeast Asia). The Chinese introduced the Japanese to many ingredients—most notably, soy sauce—as well as to techniques such as deep-frying. And some of China's favorite flavors are echoed in Korea's staple seasonings of soy, ginger, sesame, and red pepper. (Japan, too, has influenced Korean cooking: Koreans eat short-grain rice, and often serve it wrapped in or sprinkled with the dried seaweed called *nori* in Japanese, *kim* in Korean.)

Of course, China has also absorbed its share of outside influences. The curry, chiles, and highly seasoned condiments characteristic of Hunan and Szechwan cooking come from India by way of neighboring Burma. Burmese curries, like Indian ones, are generally milder than the fiery Thai and Indonesian dishes; they're offered with a choice of condiments on the side, so diners can heat up their servings as they please.

Contact with Westerners has shaped Chinese cuisine, as well. The Dutch and Portuguese traders who sailed into the commercial city of Canton introduced the Chinese to prizes from the New World: corn, potatoes, tomatoes, and peanuts.

Europeans have left a lasting mark in Southeast Asia. One of the best-known legacies comes from the Dutch colonials who settled in Indonesia: the *rijstaffel* (literally, "rice table"), a marriage of labor-intensive European serving customs and native cooking. This banquet-size meal—a multitude of Indonesian dishes centered around an enormous bowl of rice—requires hours of cooking time and dozens of waiters.

Other European and Middle Eastern traders, sailing along the China-India spice trade route, also stopped in at ports in Malaysia and Indonesia. They brought with them many of India's curry spices: coriander, cardamom, cumin, and others. These were quickly incorporated into the native cuisines, in spicy, coconut-enhanced curries.

The Philippines, under Spanish rule for centuries, still retains European culinary ties from its colonial days. Sautéing, a technique used in continental cooking, is preferred to China's speedier stir-frying. And still popular in the Philippines is an afternoon meal called *merienda*, the Asian equivalent of an English high tea. Not all the foreign influences in Filipino cooking are European, though. From the Japanese comes a preference for short-grain rice. The Chinese contribution to the culinary pool is equally apparent: noodles, soy sauce, and bean sprouts are all common ingredients. The Chinese egg roll is found here, too—in the savory Filipino treat called *lumpia*.

Indochinese (especially Vietnamese) cuisine, like that of the Philippines, illustrates the harmonious blending of European and Asian dining traditions. Though rice and noodles are the staple starches, French bread—a legacy of the French colonials—is found throughout the region. The Chinese contributed the custom of eating with chopsticks (most Southeast Asians eat with fingers or forks).

If the extent of outside influences in Oriental cuisines is striking, the smoothness with which foreign cooking ideas have been assimilated is no less impressive. Foreign techniques are applied to native ingredients and native methods to foreign foods, producing wonderful dishes which combine the best of several culinary worlds.

Crossing the Pacific

Until recent years, it was relatively simple to choose an Oriental restaurant. In most cities, you'd find just a handful of Chinese restaurants (serving mostly Cantonese food) and maybe one or two Japanese restaurants. Today's choice is more complicated. Do you want Thai food or Japanese sushi? If it's a Chinese meal you crave, from which region shall it be?

The increasing popularity of Oriental cooking is easily explained: it's a style that's in tune with modern trends toward light, healthful dining. In addition, immigration from Asian countries is on the rise. These immigrants have brought their cooking with them, and they've found an increasingly receptive audience, willing to explore and experiment with international cuisines.

Introducing Oriental Foods

Most of the 19th-century immigrants who brought Chinese cooking to the United States came from the port city of Canton. When served in its home city, Cantonese food is sophisticated and complex. But when Cantonese cooks first opened restaurants in this country, they didn't serve subtle black bean sauces or savory dim sum pastries. Instead, they offered more pedestrian fare: chop suey, egg foo yung, and sweet-and-sour stir-fries. These dishes are inexpensive and seemed likely to appeal to American tastes.

Today, the days of dimly lighted chop suey cafés and mystery-shrouded Chinatowns are gone. Oriental markets have become a place for discovery, and Asian restaurants offer an intriguing variety of cuisines and dishes. Immigrants have arrived from northern and inland Chinese cities and other Asian countries, establishing their foods and culture in cities and towns throughout North America.

Obtaining Oriental Ingredients

Increased immigration has resulted in more and better-stocked Oriental markets, including many outside major metropolitan areas. You'll also discover many authentic ingredients in well-stocked supermarkets—in fact, it's hard to find a market that *doesn't* carry fresh ginger.

However, don't let the lack of a single authentic ingredient discourage you from trying a particular recipe. In our glossary of Oriental ingredients on pages 104 to 109, we list many common substitutes for hard-to-find ingredients. And even if you can't come up with the substitute for a special spice or seasoning, don't despair—simply proceed without it. You can still capture the essence of the dish.

✳ In Your Kitchen

When you cook and serve an Oriental meal, you'll need to keep a few guidelines in mind. Apply these principles whenever you prepare Oriental food—whether you're following a recipe or trying to re-create a restaurant dish from scratch.

Slicing and Dicing

In Oriental cookery, more attention is paid to the technique of cutting than to almost any other skill. In China, the principle of balance guides cutting techniques. Beef is sliced into long slivers to complement whole pea pods; small bits of chicken match finely minced vegetables. There are practical as well as esthetic reasons for this: ingredients cut to the same size cook more evenly in a wok.

Japanese chefs are celebrated for intricate, delicate cutting methods. Whether preparing fish for sashimi or cucumbers for a salad, the cook wants the dish to look as good as it tastes. A home cook can't expect to achieve the results that trained chefs do, but do pay attention to your knife strokes and the cuts they produce.

In Southeast Asia, mortars and pestles for pounding are just as important as the knives and cleavers of Japan and China. Cooks patiently pound spices and seasonings together to achieve just the right flavor and consistency for a seasoning mixture.

If you have a blender or food processor, you needn't rely on traditional tools. Curry pastes can be mixed in seconds, and vegetables sliced with the flick of a switch. Your choice, then, is between authenticity and speed. If you're in a hurry, let beauty and tradition bow to convenience.

Styles of Dining

When you've taken the time to prepare a meal carefully, its presentation should reflect the efforts involved. Even the simplest touches—a carefully placed garnish of coriander sprigs or a lining of glossy banana leaves for a serving basket—can set an authentic mood. Look through the serving dishes illustrated on pages 102 and 103 and find items of your own that resemble the authentic pieces in size, shape, and function. You may want to invest in a set of inexpensive rice or soup bowls; either bowl can be used for both foods.

Like ethnic cuisines the world over, Asian cuisines have two distinct serving styles: one for family meals and another for banquets or special occasions. All dishes are placed on the table at once for a family-style meal; at a banquet, though, they're served in succession. If you plan to serve banquet style, arrange the menu so that both cook and guests can relax and enjoy the meal. No more than two consecutive dishes should require last-minute attention; space out the labor by serving steamed, simmered, or braised dishes between stir-fried or deep-fried dishes.

Menus for Oriental Meals

Ranging from casual to sophisticated, Oriental dishes are right for any occasion—be it an elegant buffet for a crowd or a spur-of-the-moment picnic. You'll find, too, that Oriental meals provide a satisfying answer to that oft-occurring question, "What's for dinner tonight?"

If Oriental cooking is new to you, you may want to begin by incorporating one Oriental dish into a Western menu—try Chinese stir-fried vegetables with a beef roast, for example. And you needn't limit your choice of dishes by regional or national boundaries. Base your menus on the flavor combinations you find most appealing; serve Cantonese-style vegetables before a Szechwan entrée, or Thai noodles with Korean barbecued ribs.

Chinese Picnic Lunch

Certain to delight six hungry picnickers, this savory spread is ideal for an autumn tailgate party or a springtime Sunday outing. Refrigerate the noodles and chicken salad until departure time. To keep the pork buns hot until serving time, steam them just before leaving; wrap them in heavy foil, then in six to eight layers of newspaper. Tie with string; carry it in a closed box or insulated bag.

Pork-filled Buns (page 17)
Cold-stirred Noodles (page 28)
Coriander Chicken Salad (page 29)

Chilled White Wine or Cider

Mandarin Oranges
Fortune Cookies

Appetizer Buffet

Eight lucky guests will enjoy this buffet's artful combination of flavors, textures, and temperatures (there's enough fare here for a whole meal). You can fry the won ton weeks ahead of time, freeze them, and reheat just before guests arrive.

Quail Eggs (page 109)

Fried Won Ton (page 16)

Marinated Lotus Root, Edible-pod Peas, and Carrots (page 36)

Ribs Filipino (page 92)

Marinated Abalone (page 17)

Chilled White Wine

Mongolian Grill Party

A spectacular dessert provides a dramatic finale to this cook-at-the-table meal for six. Let guests watch in anticipation as you dip bites of crisp-coated fruit into hot caramel.

Mongolian Grill (page 32)
Mandarin Pancakes (page 35)

Chilled White Wine or Beer

Caramel Fried Apples or Bananas (page 38)

Savory Supper

Here's a menu for four that's easy on the cook. You can make the dessert and the shrimp balls for the soup ahead of time; stir-fry the vegetables while the chicken rests before carving. Carve the chicken off the bones for serving—or present it in the Chinese manner, cut through the bones.

Shrimp Ball Soup (page 19)

Red-cooked Chicken (page 29)
Stir-fried Asparagus or Broccoli (page 36)
Steamed Rice (page 21)

Spicy Dinner from Szechwan

Make four chile pepper lovers happy with this spicy meal. From tangy soup to succulent shrimp, the focus is on *hot*. Steamed rice and fresh fruit help balance the peppery zest.

Hot & Sour Soup (page 19)

Szechwan Shrimp (page 25)
Steamed Rice (page 21)
Sprout & Cress Salad (page 37)

Cold Beer

Fresh Pears or Melon Wedges

Your Own Sushi Bar

If you love sushi but don't enjoy the high cost of dining in a sushi bar, this menu is just right for you. Platters of sushi and sashimi—and plenty of wasabi paste, pickled red ginger, and soy sauce for seasoning—will satisfy six to eight diners. For the sushi, you can prepare rolled (*maki*) and hand-shaped (*nigiri*) sushi ahead of time; or offer the hand-rolled (*temaki*) sushi that guests assemble themselves. Let diners choose from sashimi presented on one large or several small platters.

Rolled and Hand-shaped Sushi (pages 43 and 44)
or
Hand-rolled Sushi (page 44)
Sashimi (page 49)

Wasabi Paste (page 43), Pickled Red Ginger, and Soy Sauce

Sake and Beer

Japanese Dinner for Winter

On a blustery winter evening, warm up six chilly diners quickly with steaming simmered shellfish (*yosenabe*) and tender grilled chicken (*yakitori*); offer warm sake for sipping.

Skewered Chicken (page 51)

Simmered Shellfish (page 48)
Steamed Short-grain Rice (page 44)

Warm Sake (page 55)

Sesame or Ginger Cookies

Summertime Supper

In Japan, each season has its specialties—sturdy, warming dishes for winter, and light, cooling ones for summer. This warm-weather menu for six is ideal for patio dining or picnicking. You can prepare everything but the salmon ahead of time.

Chicken & Shrimp Noodle Salad (page 50)
Iced Sweet Onions (page 56)
Salmon Teriyaki (page 49)

Fresh Strawberries

Sukiyaki Supper

One of Japan's most popular culinary exports is *sukiyaki*, a cook-at-the-table dish of beef, noodles, and assorted vegetables. A slightly sweet soy-based braising liquid ties the various flavors together. Add a simple soup, steamed rice, and a fresh-fruit dessert, and you'll have a Japanese feast for four.

Miso Soup (page 41)

Sukiyaki (page 52)
Steamed Short-grain Rice (page 44)

Tea

Fresh Fruit

Korean Barbecue Party

Six to eight diners gather around the hibachi to cook *bul gogi* ("fire meat"), then eat it straight from the grill. Provide each diner with a bowl of rice—some to eat along with bites of meat and condiments, some to enjoy in a wrapper of toasted seaweed. Cook the pork and spinach patties just before the guests arrive.

Barbecued Beef Strips (page 70)
Pork & Spinach in Egg Batter (page 69)

Seasoned Cucumbers (page 65)
Steamed Rice in Seaweed (page 64)

Cold Beer

Korean Hot Pot Banquet

Dishes cooked and served in broth at the table are common throughout the Orient. The Korean version, *sin sul lo*, stars in this sumptuous feast for six. The supporting cast includes spicy *kim chee*, mild-flavored fish, and ripe fresh fruit.

Fried Fish Squares (page 69)
Sesame Dipping Sauce (page 69)

Korean Hot Pot (page 68)
Steamed Short-grain Rice (page 44)
Cabbage Pickles with Daikon (page 65)

Butter Cookies
Fresh Persimmons or Plums

Southeast Asian Sampler

At your next cocktail party, tempt 10 to 12 guests with an array of exotic finger foods. You may want to delegate a satay cook to grill the skewered chicken (or let guests cook their own). Plan on passing the Imperial Rolls; everything else can be served buffet style. Imperial Rolls can be cooked and frozen weeks ahead; Peanut Sauce can be prepared a day ahead (double the recipe, and use the sauce as a dip for both satay and shrimp chips).

Imperial Rolls (page 75)

Beef Chiang Mai (page 91)

Singapore Satay (page 86)
Peanut Sauce (page 92)

Shrimp Chips (page 95)

Cucumbers with Tomato Relish (page 75)

Vietnamese Hot Pot Dinner

Like fondue, a hot pot offers diners a festive, "hands-on" approach to dining. All the ingredients for Simmered Beef in Rice Paper can be prepared ahead, freeing the cook to enjoy the meal with five other diners.

Chicken with Mint (page 86)

Simmered Beef in Rice Paper (page 90)

Fresh Fruit

Nut or Butter Cookies

Indonesian Rijstaffel

Most modern cooks have neither the time nor the manpower for a traditional rijstaffel (as known under the Dutch colonials), an elaborate banquet of 20 to 30 dishes. But you can still capture the variety and abundance essential to a true rijstaffel in this scaled-down version—a festive menu for eight.

Chicken Soup with Condiments (page 76)

Dry Beef Curry (page 91)
Sour Vegetables (page 95)
Steamed Rice (page 21) or
Festive Yellow Rice (page 78)

Banana Fritters (page 97)

Simple Thai Supper

Here's a menu that's right for a family dinner or a small dinner party. Begin with crisp greens bathed in a warm and spicy dressing; then bring on the spicy, coconutty curry. (There's plenty of sauce, so be sure to provide lots of rice alongside.) Sweet and succulent fresh pineapple brings this meal for four to a refreshing close.

Wilted Romaine with Hot Sausage Dressing (page 94)

Thai Red Curry (page 88)
Steamed Rice (page 21)

Fresh Pineapple

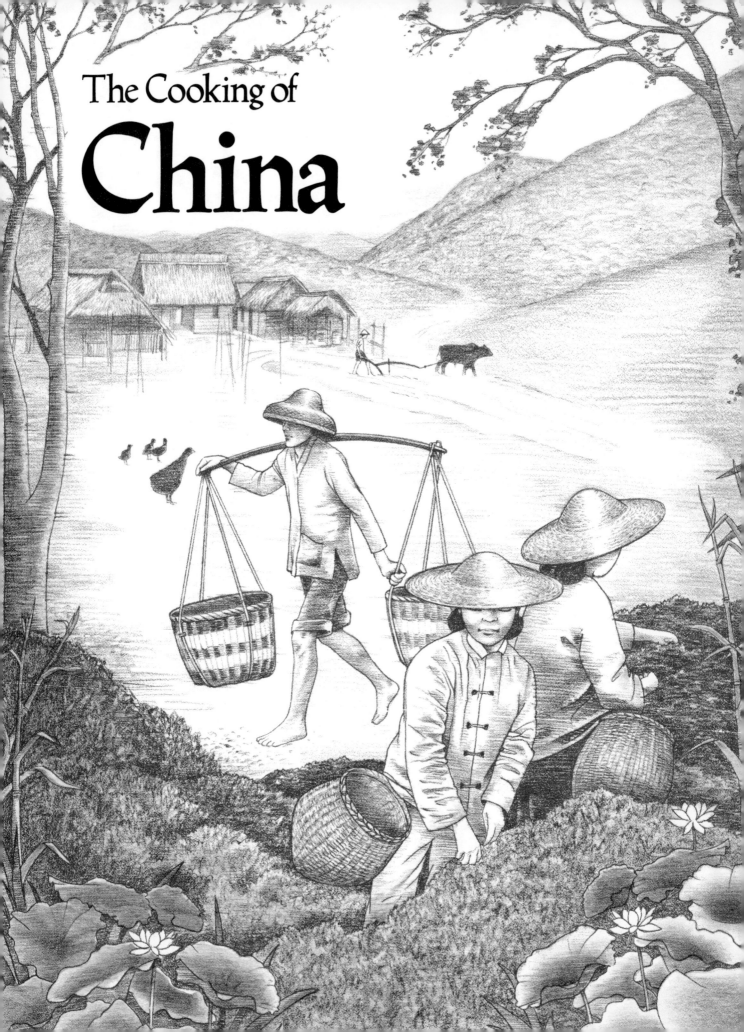

The Cooking of
China

Chinese cuisine falls into four distinct styles—each associated with a particular geographic region, and each with its own characteristic ingredients and flavors.

Peking, in the north, has been a government and trade center during much of China's history. Its cooking style is sophisticated, featuring dishes flavored with sesame oil, spicy hoisin, and soy. Wheat—eaten in the form of pancakes, buns, and noodles—is the staple starch here.

Shanghai style is subtle and complex. "Red-cooked" dishes—foods braised in a soy-based cooking liquid—and delicate seafood typify the cuisine of this industrial port city on the eastern coast.

South of Shanghai lies the coastal city of Canton. Fresh seafood, fruits, and vegetables are all abundant here, and Canton style stresses fresh, natural flavors. Foods are often seasoned only lightly, with the mildest of sauces. Specialties of the area include colorful stir-fries and dim sum delicacies.

Szechwan and Hunan provinces, in the southeast, are noted for their spicy-hot dishes (Hunan style is the hotter of the two). Chiles grow well in this region's semitropical climate, and they're used lavishly in cooking.

Appetizers

Pot Stickers

Pot stickers (*guotie*) look like they'll stick to the cooking pan—but in fact, they lift out easily with a spatula. Assembly goes quickly, since you use purchased wrappers. Labeled as *gyoza* (their Japanese name), they're sold alongside won ton skins in well-stocked supermarkets and Oriental markets.

> Pork & Shrimp Filling (recipe follows)
> 1 package (14 oz.) pot sticker wrappers
> ¼ cup salad oil
> 1⅓ cups regular-strength chicken broth
> Soy sauce
> Vinegar
> Chili oil

Prepare Pork & Shrimp Filling.

To assemble each pot sticker, place 2 rounded teaspoons of the filling in center of a wrapper. Moisten edge of dough with water, then fold wrapper in half over filling to form a semicircle. Starting at one end, pinch curved edges closed; as you seal edges, make 3 evenly spaced decorative tucks along edge facing you. When entire curve is sealed, turn pot sticker seam side up; then set it down firmly, so it will sit flat. Cover while shaping remaining pot stickers.

(At this point, you may arrange pot stickers in a single layer on a baking sheet, then cover and freeze until firm. Transfer to plastic bags and return to freezer; freeze for up to 4 weeks. Cook, without thawing, as directed below.)

Cook pot stickers 12 at a time. For each batch, heat 1 tablespoon of the salad oil in a wide, heavy frying pan over medium heat. Set pot stickers, seam side up, in pan. Cook until bottoms are golden brown (8 to 10 minutes). Pour in ⅓ cup of the broth and immediately cover pan tightly. Reduce heat to low; cook for 10 minutes (15 minutes if frozen). Uncover and continue cooking until all liquid is absorbed. Using a wide spatula, transfer pot stickers, browned side up, to a heatproof platter. Cover and keep warm in a 200° oven. Repeat with remaining salad oil, pot stickers, and broth.

Serve hot; offer soy, vinegar, and chili oil on the side. Makes about 48 pot stickers.

Near a hillside village, Chinese farm workers harvest tea leaves from bushy shrubs.

(Continued on next page)

Pork & Shrimp Filling. Chop ½ pound **medium-size shrimp,** shelled and deveined. Place in a bowl; then add ½ pound **ground pork,** 1 cup finely chopped **cabbage,** ¼ cup *each* minced **green onions** (including tops) and chopped **mushrooms,** 2 tablespoons **oyster sauce** or soy sauce, and 1 clove **garlic,** minced or pressed.

Fried Won Ton
(Pictured on front cover)

Won ton make delightful party fare; each bite-size dumpling is a crisp, crunchy deep-fried wrapper enclosing a savory filling. Keep them on hand in the freezer, ready to re-heat for spur-of-the-moment festivities.

　　Hot Mustard (recipe follows)
1　pound ground pork or ½ pound *each* ground pork and medium-size shrimp, shelled, deveined, and finely chopped
⅓　cup water chestnuts, finely chopped
2　green onions (including tops), finely chopped
1　tablespoon soy sauce
½　teaspoon salt
⅛　teaspoon pepper
½　teaspoon minced fresh ginger
2　teaspoons dry sherry
1　egg
1　package (1 lb.) won ton skins
　　Salad oil
　　Catsup

Prepare Hot Mustard and set aside.

　　Combine pork, water chestnuts, onions, soy, salt, pepper, ginger, and sherry; mix well. In a small bowl, beat egg lightly.

　　Place 1 won ton skin on countertop or other flat surface; cover remaining skins with a damp towel to keep them pliable. Mound 1 teaspoon of the pork filling in one corner. Fold that corner over filling, and roll to tuck point under (see photos on page 18). Moisten the 2 side corners with egg; bring together, overlapping slightly. Pinch together firmly to seal. Repeat with remaining skins, placing filled won ton slightly apart on a baking sheet; cover.

　　If you're making won ton for Won Ton Soup (page 19), you may prepare them to this point, then cover and refrigerate for up to 8 hours. Or, for longer storage, freeze on baking sheet until firm; then transfer to plastic bags and return to freezer. Do not freeze uncooked won ton if you intend to deep-fry them.

　　Into a deep, heavy pan at least 6 inches in diameter, pour oil to a depth of 2 inches and heat to 360° on a deep-frying thermometer. Add 4 to 6 won ton and cook, turning occasionally, until golden brown (about 2 minutes). Remove with a slotted spoon and drain on paper towels. Keep warm in a 200° oven. Repeat with remaining won ton. Serve with Hot Mustard and catsup.

　　If made ahead, let cool; then place in plastic bags and freeze for up to 4 weeks. To reheat, arrange frozen won ton in a single layer on a baking sheet and heat in a 350° oven for about 12 minutes or until heated through. Makes 6 to 7 dozen won ton.

Hot Mustard. Place ¼ cup **dry mustard** in a small bowl. Stirring constantly, slowly pour in ¼ cup **cold water;** continue to stir until mixture is smooth. Stir in ⅛ teaspoon **salad oil.** Cover and let stand for 1 hour. Makes about ⅓ cup.

Barbecued Pork

You'll probably want to keep versatile Cantonese *char siu* on hand in the freezer. It's a tasty appetizer or snack, and it adds wonderful flavor to Won Ton Soup (page 19) and Fried Rice (page 21).

¼　cup soy sauce
2　tablespoons *each* honey, sugar, and dry sherry
1　teaspoon salt
1　teaspoon Chinese five-spice or ¼ teaspoon *each* crushed anise seeds and ground cinnamon, cloves, and ginger
3　quarter-size slices fresh ginger, crushed
3　pounds lean boneless pork (butt or leg)

In a small pan, combine soy, honey, sugar, sherry, salt, five-spice, and ginger. Heat over medium heat for 1 minute to dissolve sugar; let cool.

　　Cut pork into 1-inch-thick slices; place in a plastic bag and pour in marinade. Seal bag and refrigerate for at least 4 hours or until next day, turning occasionally to distribute marinade.

　　Drain pork, reserving marinade, and place on a rack set over a foil-lined baking pan. Bake in a 350° oven for 30 minutes. Turn pieces over and bake for 45 more minutes, brushing occasionally with reserved marinade. Cut into thin slices; serve hot or cold. Makes about 2½ pounds.

Marinated Abalone

Fresh abalone is hard to find in the U.S., so we've used canned abalone in this simple salad.

> 1 teaspoon sesame seeds
> 2 tablespoons *each* white (distilled) vinegar and water
> 3 tablespoons soy sauce
> 1 teaspoon sugar
> 1 green onion (including top), thinly sliced
> Dash of ground red pepper (cayenne)
> 1 can (about 8 oz.) abalone

In a small frying pan over medium heat, toast sesame seeds, shaking pan frequently, until golden (about 2 minutes). Remove pan from heat and stir in vinegar, water, soy, sugar, onion, and pepper.

Drain abalone, then thinly slice. Place in a plastic bag and pour in marinade. Seal bag and refrigerate for at least 2 hours, turning occasionally. Drain and arrange on a serving dish. Makes 6 to 8 servings.

Spiced Chicken Livers

A soy-based cooking liquid lends rich flavor and deep mahogany color to braised chicken livers.

> 1 pound chicken livers
> Water
> ½ cup soy sauce
> ¼ cup dry sherry
> 1 tablespoon sugar
> ½ whole star anise or ½ teaspoon anise seeds
> 1 cinnamon stick (about 1 inch long)
> 1 quarter-size slice fresh ginger, crushed
> 1 green onion (including top), cut into 1-inch lengths
> ¼ teaspoon crushed red pepper (optional)

Place livers in a 2-quart pan and pour in water to cover. Bring just to boiling over high heat; drain. Add soy, ½ cup water, sherry, sugar, anise, cinnamon stick, ginger, onion, and, if desired, pepper. Then cover, reduce heat, and simmer for 15 minutes. Remove from heat and let cool.

Cut livers into bite-size pieces. Return to cooking liquid; cover and refrigerate for 1 hour or up to 2 days. Drain; discard ginger and onion. Arrange livers in a serving dish. Makes 6 to 8 servings.

Dining on Dim Sum

Dim sum is a traditional Cantonese teahouse meal of small, savory treats. *Bow*—pork-filled buns—are typical dim sum offerings.

Pork-filled Buns

> 1 package active dry yeast
> 1 cup warm water (about 110°)
> ⅓ cup sugar
> 2 tablespoons salad oil
> 1 teaspoon salt
> About 3¼ cups unsifted all-purpose flour
> Pork Filling (recipe follows)

Dissolve yeast in water; blend in sugar, oil, and salt. Let stand in a warm place until bubbly (about 15 minutes). Add 3¼ cups of the flour and mix until dough holds together. Place on a lightly floured board; knead until smooth and elastic (8 to 10 minutes). Place in a greased bowl, cover, and let rise in a warm place until doubled (about 1¼ hours). Meanwhile, prepare Pork Filling.

Turn dough out onto a lightly floured board and knead for 1 minute. Shape into a rectangle, then cut rectangle into 12 equal pieces

Roll each piece into a 4½-inch round; press edges to make them slightly thinner than rest of round. Place 2 tablespoons of filling on each round. Pull edges of dough up around filling; twist to seal.

Place each bun, sealed side down, on a 3-inch square of foil. Cover and let rise in a warm place until puffy and light (about 30 minutes). Set in a steamer over boiling water. Cover and steam until tops are glazed and smooth (12 to 15 minutes). Serve warm; or let cool, wrap airtight, and freeze for up to 4 weeks. To reheat, steam frozen buns until hot (about 10 minutes). Makes 12 buns.

Pork Filling. Cut 1½ pounds **lean boneless pork** into ½-inch cubes. Place in a bowl; add 2 cloves **garlic,** minced or pressed, ½ teaspoon grated **fresh ginger,** 2 teaspoons **sugar,** and 2 tablespoons **soy sauce.** In another bowl, combine 2 teaspoons **sugar,** 1 tablespoon **cornstarch,** 2 tablespoons **soy sauce,** 1 tablespoon **dry sherry,** and ¼ cup **water.**

Heat 1 tablespoon **salad oil** in a wok or wide frying pan over high heat. Add pork and stir-fry until browned (about 5 minutes). Add 1 medium-size **onion,** chopped, and stir-fry until soft (about 2 minutes). Stir cornstarch mixture, then add; cook, stirring, until sauce boils and thickens. Let cool.

Won Ton Soup *(Recipe on facing page)*

1 Mound pork filling on lower corner of won ton skin. Fold that corner over filling; roll to tuck point under.

2 Moisten two side corners with egg; pull them together behind filled corner (away from exposed upper corner) and overlap slightly.

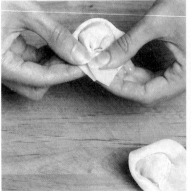

3 Pinch ends firmly together to seal. Place filled won ton on a baking sheet; keep covered while you fill and fold remaining won ton.

4 Boil filled won ton before adding to hot soup. Drain well before transferring to steaming broth.

 # Soups

Won Ton Soup
(Pictured on facing page)

The Chinese add substance and flavor to simple chicken soup with the small filled dumplings known as *won ton*. Filling and folding the wrappers may go slowly at first, but take heart—speed and agility come with practice.

  36 uncooked won ton (page 16)
    6 cups regular-strength chicken broth
    2 cups thickly sliced napa cabbage or bok choy
    3 green onions (including tops), thinly sliced
    1 cup slivered Barbecued Pork (page 16)
    1 teaspoon soy sauce
  ½ teaspoon sesame oil

Fill a large kettle with water and bring to a boil over high heat. Drop in won ton; then reduce heat and simmer, uncovered, until pork in filling is no longer pink (about 4 minutes; 6 minutes if frozen).

Meanwhile, pour broth into a 3 to 4-quart pan and bring to a boil over medium-high heat. Add cabbage and onions and cook for 3 minutes. Remove won ton from water with a slotted spoon and drop into hot broth. Add pork, soy, and oil and cook until pork is heated through. Makes 6 servings.

Shrimp Ball Soup

This fresh-tasting soup from Peking is as eye-catching as it's tasty: delicately seasoned broth holds bright green edible-pod peas, fluffy pink shrimp balls, and translucent bean threads. You can prepare the shrimp balls several days ahead.

      Shrimp Balls (recipe follows)
    2 ounces bean threads
    4 cups regular-strength chicken broth
    1 teaspoon *each* dry sherry and soy sauce
  ¼ pound mushrooms, thinly sliced
  20 edible-pod peas, ends and strings removed
    3 sprigs fresh coriander (cilantro)
      Salt

Prepare Shrimp Balls; set aside.

Soak bean threads in warm water to cover for 30 minutes. Drain, then cut into 6-inch lengths.

Pour broth into a 2-quart pan; add sherry and soy. Place over medium-high heat and bring just to boiling. Add bean threads and mushrooms; reduce heat and simmer, uncovered, for 5 minutes. Add peas and cook for 2 minutes. Add Shrimp Balls; cook just until heated through. Garnish with coriander; season to taste with salt. Makes 4 to 6 servings.

Shrimp Balls. In a bowl, beat 1 **egg white** until foamy. In another bowl, stir together 2 teaspoons *each* **dry sherry** and **cornstarch;** add to egg white along with ½ teaspoon *each* **salt** and grated **fresh ginger.** Mix in ¼ cup **water chestnuts,** finely chopped, and ½ pound **medium-size shrimp,** shelled, deveined, and finely chopped. Coat hands with **salad oil;** roll shrimp mixture into walnut-size balls. Heat a 2 to 3-quart pan of **water** to simmering. Drop in a few shrimp balls and simmer until they float (4 to 5 minutes); lift out with a slotted spoon. Repeat until all are cooked. If made ahead, let cool; cover and refrigerate for up to 2 days.

Hot & Sour Soup

Give your meal a spicy start with this tongue-tickling soup from Szechwan. Pepper provides the heat; vinegar adds the sour tang.

    4 medium-size Oriental dried mushrooms
  ¼ pound lean boneless pork (butt or leg), cut into matchstick pieces
    1 tablespoon dry sherry
    4 cups regular-strength chicken broth
  ½ pound chicken breast, skinned, boned, and cut into matchstick pieces
  ½ cup sliced bamboo shoots, cut into matchstick pieces
  ¼ pound medium-firm tofu (bean curd), drained and cut into ½-inch cubes
    2 tablespoons white wine vinegar
    1 tablespoon soy sauce
    2 tablespoons cornstarch
  ¼ cup water
  ½ to ¾ teaspoon white pepper
    1 teaspoon sesame oil
    1 egg
    2 green onions (including tops), cut diagonally into 1-inch slices
      Salt

(Continued on next page)

Soak mushrooms in warm water to cover for 30 minutes; drain. Cut off and discard stems; thinly slice caps. Combine pork with sherry; let stand for 10 minutes.

Pour broth into a 2-quart pan and bring to a boil over medium-high heat. Add mushrooms, pork, chicken, and bamboo shoots. Stir several times; then cover, reduce heat, and simmer for 5 minutes. Add tofu, vinegar, and soy; heat, uncovered, for 1 minute. In a small bowl, stir together cornstarch and water. Pour into pan and cook, stirring, until thickened. Remove from heat; stir in pepper and oil.

In a small bowl, lightly beat egg; slowly pour into soup, stirring constantly. Sprinkle with onions and season to taste with salt. Makes 6 servings.

Bean Curd & Eggs

Spicy Bean Curd

A fiery sauce coats cubes of delicate tofu in this succulent stir-fry. To balance its zestiness—and soothe your palate—serve plain steamed rice alongside.

- ½ to ⅔ **pound medium-firm tofu (bean curd)**
- 1 **teaspoon** *each* **soy sauce and dry sherry**
- 1 **teaspoon sweet bean sauce or hoisin sauce**
- ¼ **pound ground pork**
- 3 **tablespoons salad oil**
- 1 **teaspoon minced fresh ginger**
- 2 **teaspoons minced garlic**
- 2 **teaspoons hot bean sauce or 2 small dried whole hot red chiles (crumbled and seeded, if desired)**
- ¾ **cup water**
- 2 **tablespoons soy sauce**
- 2 **green onions (including tops), thinly sliced**
- 2 **tablespoons** *each* **water and cornstarch**

Cut tofu into ½-inch cubes; place in a colander and let drain for 15 minutes. In a bowl, blend the 1 teaspoon soy, sherry, and sweet bean sauce; add pork and stir to coat. Stir in 1 teaspoon of the oil; let marinate for 15 minutes.

Heat a wok or wide frying pan over high heat. When pan is hot, add remaining oil. When oil be-

gins to heat, add ginger and garlic. Stir once, then add pork and stir-fry until meat is no longer pink (about 2 minutes). Stir in hot bean sauce. Add tofu, the ¾ cup water, and the 2 tablespoons soy. Cook for 3 minutes; then add onions. Stir together the 2 tablespoons water and cornstarch; pour into pan and cook, stirring, until sauce boils and thickens. Makes 2 or 3 servings.

Shrimp Egg Foo Yung

Laced with shrimp and crunchy vegetables and topped with a savory sauce, these colorful egg patties from Canton make a quick and delicious entrée.

- ¼ **pound green beans, ends removed**
  About ¼ cup salad oil
- 1 **clove garlic, minced**
- ¼ **pound medium-size shrimp, shelled, deveined, and coarsely chopped**
- 1 **carrot, shredded**
  Foo Yung Sauce (recipe follows)
- 6 **eggs**
- 1 **teaspoon salt**
- ¼ **teaspoon white pepper**

Cut beans crosswise into ⅛-inch slanting slices; set aside. Heat a wide frying pan over high heat. When pan is hot, add 2 tablespoons of the oil. When oil begins to heat, add garlic. Stir once, then add shrimp and stir-fry for 1 minute. Add beans and carrot, reduce heat to medium, and stir-fry until beans are tender-crisp to bite (about 2 minutes). Remove from pan and let cool.

Prepare Foo Yung Sauce and keep hot. In a bowl, beat eggs with salt and pepper; then stir in shrimp-vegetable mixture.

Heat 2 more tablespoons oil in pan over medium-high heat. When oil is hot, pour egg mixture into pan in ¼-cup portions; shape each portion into a patty (cook 3 or 4 at a time). Cook, turning once, until golden on both sides. Remove to a heated platter; keep warm. Repeat with remaining egg mixture, adding more oil as needed. Pour hot sauce over patties and serve at once. Makes 6 servings.

Foo Yung Sauce. In a pan, heat 1 cup **regular-strength chicken broth,** 1 tablespoon **soy sauce,** and 2 teaspoons *each* **sugar** and **vinegar.** Stir together 1 tablespoon **cornstarch** and 2 tablespoons **water.** Pour into pan and cook, stirring, until sauce boils and thickens.

Chinese Hat

A softly cooked omelet "hat" conceals a mound of pork and vegetables in this unusual entrée.

- 12 **Mandarin Pancakes (page 35)**
- 5 **Oriental dried mushrooms**
- ⅓ **cup dried tiger lily buds**
- 1 **tablespoon cornstarch**
- ½ **cup regular-strength chicken broth**
- 2 **tablespoons** *each* **oyster sauce and dry sherry**
- 1 **tablespoon white wine vinegar**
- 6 **eggs**
- 2 **tablespoons water**
- ¾ **pound ground pork**
- 1 **onion, chopped**
- 1 **clove garlic, minced or pressed**
- ¼ **pound bean sprouts**
- ¼ **teaspoon crushed red pepper (optional)**
- 3 **tablespoons chopped fresh coriander (cilantro)**
- 2 **tablespoons butter or margarine**

Prepare Mandarin Pancakes and set aside.

Soak mushrooms and lily buds in warm water to cover for 30 minutes; drain. Cut off and discard mushroom stems; cut caps into thin strips. Pinch off and discard hard tips from lily buds, then cut buds in half lengthwise. Set aside.

Heat pancakes for serving as directed on page 35. In a small bowl, combine cornstarch and broth; stir in oyster sauce, sherry, and vinegar. Set aside. In another bowl, beat eggs with water; set aside.

Crumble pork into a wok or wide frying pan over medium-high heat; cook, stirring, until browned. Remove with a slotted spoon. Add onion and garlic to drippings; cook, stirring, until soft. Add mushrooms, lily buds, and bean sprouts and cook, stirring, for 1 minute. Return pork to pan and sprinkle with pepper (if used). Stir broth mixture, then pour into pan. Cook, stirring, until mixture boils and thickens. Remove from heat; mound on a serving plate. Sprinkle with coriander; keep warm.

Melt butter in a 9½ to 10½-inch omelet pan (or frying pan with rounded sides and a nonstick finish) over medium heat. Heat until foam begins to subside; then pour in egg mixture all at once. As edges begin to set, lift with a spatula and shake or tilt pan to let uncooked egg flow underneath. When egg is set but surface is still moist, use a thin-bladed spatula to nudge omelet (without folding it) toward edge of pan. Slip omelet onto meat mixture.

To serve, spoon egg and meat onto a pancake; roll up and eat out of hand. Makes 4 to 6 servings.

Rice, Chinese Style

Chinese-style rice isn't always plain and unseasoned. Fried rice—cooked rice stir-fried with bits of meat and vegetables and flavored with soy—is a popular snack in China; you can serve it as a speedy and nutritious one-dish meal. There's only one requirement for successful fried rice: start with *cold* cooked rice. If the rice isn't cold to begin with, the grains won't stay separate.

Steamed Rice

Place 1¼ cups **long-grain rice** in a 2-quart pan. Add water to cover; stir well and drain. Repeat until water runs clear. To drained rice, add 1¾ cups **cold water** and, if desired, **salt** to taste. Place over medium-high heat and bring to a boil; boil, uncovered, until bubbles disappear from surface and only a thin film of water covers top of rice (about 8 minutes). Cover pan, reduce heat to low, and cook until rice is tender to bite (about 20 minutes). Remove from heat and let stand for at least 5 minutes or up to 30 minutes. Fluff with a fork. Makes 4 cups.

Fried Rice

- **Steamed Rice (above)**
- 2 **eggs**
- ¼ **teaspoon salt**
- 4 **tablespoons salad oil**
- 2 **green onions (including tops), thinly sliced**
- 1 **cup small cooked shrimp or 1 cup diced Barbecued Pork (page 16) or cooked ham**
- ½ **cup frozen peas, thawed**
- ½ **cup roasted cashews**
- 2 **tablespoons soy sauce**

Prepare Steamed Rice; let cool, then refrigerate until cold.

Rub cold rice with wet hands so all grains are separated; set aside.

In a bowl, beat eggs with salt. In a wok or wide frying pan, heat 1 tablespoon of the oil over medium heat. Add onions and stir-fry for about 30 seconds. Add eggs; cook and stir until softly set. Remove from pan and set aside.

Heat 1 more tablespoon oil in pan. Add shrimp, peas, and cashews. Stir-fry for 2 minutes to heat through; remove from pan and set aside. Heat remaining 2 tablespoons oil in pan. Add rice and stir-fry for 2 minutes to heat through. Stir in soy and shrimp mixture. Add eggs; stir mixture gently until eggs are in small pieces. Makes 4 or 5 servings.

Fish & Shellfish

Sweet & Sour Deep-fried Fish

A Cantonese classic, *teem seen shek bon* pairs crisp fried fish with a tart-sweet sauce. Often served on special occasions, this dish has symbolic significance: the whole fish stands for totality, and the red color of the sauce for good luck.

> Sweet & Sour Sauce (recipe follows)
> 1 **whole mild-flavored, white-fleshed fish, such as red snapper or rock cod, cleaned and scaled (2 to 2½ lbs.)**
> ¼ **cup dry sherry**
> **About ½ cup cornstarch**
> **Salad oil**
> 1 **small green pepper, slivered**
> 1 **small tomato, cut into 6 wedges**
> **Fresh coriander (cilantro) sprigs**

Prepare Sweet & Sour Sauce; set aside.

Rinse fish and pat dry. With a sharp knife, make about six ½-inch-deep diagonal slashes across each side of fish. Rub fish all over with sherry; then coat heavily with cornstarch, patting it on.

Half-fill a wok or wide frying pan with oil and heat to 380° on a deep-frying thermometer. Slowly slide fish into oil. (Oil temperature will drop; adjust heat to stabilize temperature at 360°.) Cook fish until golden brown (about 5 minutes); if fish isn't completely immersed in oil, spoon hot oil over fish as it cooks.

With a large wire strainer or 2 slotted spatulas, carefully lift fish from oil. Drain briefly, then place on a rimmed platter and keep warm in a 200° oven for up to 15 minutes.

Place Sweet & Sour Sauce over high heat; heat, stirring, until bubbly. Stir in green pepper and tomato. Pour sauce around (not over) fish on platter. Garnish with coriander sprigs. Lift portions of fish onto plates; spoon sauce over top. Makes 3 to 6 servings.

Sweet & Sour Sauce. Heat 2 tablespoons **salad oil** in a 2 to 3-quart pan over medium-high heat. Add 1 small **onion**, sliced and separated into rings; cook, stirring, for 1 minute. Stir in ½ cup *each* **catsup, red wine vinegar,** and **unsweetened pineapple juice;** then add ¾ cup **sugar,** ½ teaspoon **Worcestershire,** and ⅛ teaspoon **liquid hot pepper seasoning.** Combine 2 tablespoons *each* **cornstarch** and **water** and stir in. Cook, stirring, until sauce boils, thickens, and turns clear (about 2 minutes). If made ahead, cover and set aside for up to 4 hours.

Trout with Ginger
(Pictured on facing page)

In this recipe, fish cooks by an innovative technique that we call "steeping." Based on a classic Chinese cooking method, steeping doesn't rely on direct heat; instead, it uses only the warmth retained in water that's brought to a boil, then removed from the heat. Fish prepared this way is exceptionally moist, smooth textured, and evenly cooked. Bathe the succulent fish in a light ginger and garlic sauce before serving.

> 4 **whole cleaned trout (2 to 3 lbs. *total*)**
> 3 **quarter-size slices fresh ginger**
> 2 **tablespoons soy sauce**
> ⅓ **cup 1-inch slivers green onions (including tops)**
> 2 **pounds spinach, stems removed, rinsed well**
> ¼ **cup salad oil**
> 2 **cloves garlic, minced**
> 2 **tablespoons 1-inch slivers fresh ginger**

Rinse trout and pat dry with paper towels. Place in a wide frying pan or 5 to 6-quart kettle; then pour in water to cover fish by 1 to 2 inches. Lift out fish and set aside. Add ginger slices to water. Cover pan and bring water to a full rolling boil over high heat.

Turn off heat; then immediately immerse fish in water. Cover pan tightly; do not uncover until ready to test for doneness. Let fish steep until flesh inside looks opaque (about 8 minutes per inch of thickness measured at thickest portion—to test, slash in thickest portion with a knife).

Lift fish from pan and drain; place on a platter. Drizzle with soy; sprinkle with onion. Plunge spinach into hot water fish has steeped in and stir until wilted (1 to 2 minutes). Drain and arrange around fish. Heat oil in a small pan over medium heat. Add garlic and ginger slivers and cook just until garlic is light golden (about 1 minute); pour over fish. Makes 4 servings.

Trout with Ginger *(Recipe on facing page)*

1 When water reaches a full rolling boil, turn off heat. Arrange fish in pan; cover tightly and let steep.

2 To check for doneness, lift fish from water and slash thickest portion with a knife. Fish is cooked when flesh looks opaque.

3 Plunge spinach into fish steeping liquid. Remaining heat will cook greens; stir just until wilted.

4 Drizzle hot oil, flavored with ginger and garlic, over platter of succulent fish and spinach.

Steamed Fish with Clams

The Chinese choice for steamed fish is a *whole* fish: to Chinese cooks, a fish looks incomplete without its head and tail. And if you use a whole fish, you can enjoy the tender bits of flesh around the cheeks and tail (the Chinese consider these the choicest morsels of all). Of course, you can use fillets if you prefer—the gentle steam heat cooks them beautifully, too.

> 1 or 2 whole mild-flavored, white-fleshed fish, such as rockfish, red snapper, or kingfish, cleaned and scaled (1½ to 2½ lbs. *total*); or 1½ pounds fillets, such as rockfish, turbot, sole, or sea bass
> 2 teaspoons salt
> 3 quarter-size slices fresh ginger
> 12 small live hard-shell clams, scrubbed
> 4 green onions (including tops)
> 2 to 3 tablespoons salad oil
> 5 sprigs fresh coriander (cilantro)
> 2 tablespoons matchstick pieces fresh ginger
> 2 tablespoons soy sauce

With a sharp knife, make three ½-inch-deep diagonal slashes across each side of fish. Rub fish inside and out with salt. (If you use fillets, decrease salt to 1 teaspoon; rub over all sides of fillets.) Place fish on a heatproof dish or platter that will fit inside a large steamer. Place ginger slices on fish; arrange clams on dish around fish.

Cut 2 of the onions into 1½-inch pieces and place on fish. (At this point, you may cover and refrigerate for up to 4 hours; bring to room temperature before steaming.) Cut remaining 2 onions into 1½-inch lengths, then slice lengthwise into thin shreds; set aside.

Place dish on rack in steamer. Cover and steam over boiling water until clams open and flesh inside fish looks opaque—8 to 10 minutes for small fish or fillets, 10 to 12 minutes for a 1½-pound fish, and 16 to 18 minutes for a 2½-pound fish. To test, prod in thickest portion with a fork. (If you're cooking a large fish, remove clams after they open and keep warm; return to serving dish after draining off cooking liquid.) While fish is cooking, heat oil in a small pan over medium-low heat until hot but not smoking (use larger amount of oil for large fish).

Remove dish with fish from steamer; discard ginger slices and onion pieces. Tip dish slightly to drain off cooking liquid. Sprinkle onion shreds, coriander, matchstick pieces ginger, and soy over fish. Pour hot oil over fish just before serving. For easier serving, slide a second dish under hot cooking dish before bringing fish to the table. Makes 3 to 6 servings.

Lobster Cantonese

Lobster Cantonese is, of course, traditionally made with lobster—so the savory sauce that characterizes this dish is often called "lobster sauce." Don't hesitate to break with tradition, though; the sauce is delightful with crab, shrimp, and scallops, too.

> Cooking Sauce (recipe follows)
> 1½ pounds raw lobster tails (thaw if frozen)
> 1 egg
> 3 tablespoons salad oil
> 2 tablespoons fermented black beans, rinsed, drained, and finely chopped
> 2 cloves garlic, minced
> 1 teaspoon minced fresh ginger
> ¼ pound ground pork
> 1 green onion (including top), thinly sliced

Prepare Cooking Sauce and set aside. If you want to cook lobster in the shell, trim side fins; cut tails in half lengthwise and devein (if large, cut in half crosswise). Or remove meat from shells and cut into bite-size pieces. In a small bowl, lightly beat egg.

Heat a wok or wide frying pan over high heat. When pan is hot, add oil. When oil begins to heat, add beans, garlic, and ginger. Stir once; add pork and stir-fry until no longer pink (about 2 minutes).

Add lobster and cook, stirring constantly, until shells turn red or until shelled meat is opaque throughout (3 to 4 minutes). Stir Cooking Sauce, pour into pan, and cook, stirring, until sauce boils and thickens. Add onion and egg; stir until egg begins to set (about 30 seconds). Makes 3 or 4 servings.

Cooking Sauce. In a small bowl, stir together 1 tablespoon *each* **cornstarch, soy sauce,** and **dry sherry;** ½ cup **regular-strength chicken broth;** and a dash of **white pepper.**

Crab Cantonese

Follow directions for **Lobster Cantonese,** but use 1 **large cooked crab** (1½ to 2 pounds), cleaned and cracked, in place of lobster. Cut body in quarters; leave legs and claws whole. Cook crab until heated through (3 to 4 minutes).

Shrimp Cantonese

Follow directions for **Lobster Cantonese,** but use 1 pound **medium-size shrimp** in place of lobster. Cut through back of shell with scissors and devein, or remove shells and devein. Cook shrimp until they turn pink (about 3 minutes).

Scallops Cantonese

Follow directions for **Lobster Cantonese,** but use 1 pound **scallops,** cut into ¼-inch-thick slices, in place of lobster. Cook scallops until opaque throughout (about 3 minutes).

Stir-fried Squid & Peas

Before cooking, tender squid is scored in a cross-hatched pattern. In addition to looking decorative, the crisscross cuts encourage rapid, even cooking.

  1 **pound squid**
  2 **tablespoons salad oil**
  ½ **teaspoon minced fresh ginger**
  1 **cup frozen peas, thawed**
  ½ **cup regular-strength chicken broth**
  1 **teaspoon soy sauce**
  1 **tablespoon oyster sauce**
  ¼ **teaspoon sugar**
  2 **teaspoons cornstarch**
  1 **tablespoon water**

Clean squid. To do this, first peel off and discard transparent speckled membrane from hood, exposing white meat of hood. Pull out and discard long, transparent, sword-shaped shell from inside hood. Holding hood in one hand and body (with tentacles) in the other, pull gently on body to separate it from hood.

Squeeze out and discard contents of hood; rinse inside. Strip off and discard any material that separates easily from body, including ink sac. If ink sac breaks, rinse body to remove ink. Turn body upside down so tentacles are spread open. Squeeze gently to pop out hard, parrotlike beak from between tentacles. Discard beak. Cut tentacles from body and set aside; discard rest of body. Slit hood lengthwise and open flat. With a knife, make diagonal cuts ½ inch apart across inside of hood. Repeat in opposite direction so knife marks look like crosshatching. Cut hood into pieces about 2 inches square. Wash squares and tentacles, drain, and pat dry.

Heat a wok or wide frying pan over medium-high heat. When pan is hot, add 1 tablespoon of the oil. When oil begins to heat, add ginger and stir once. Add squid squares and tentacles and stir-fry just until edges of squares curl (1½ to 2 minutes). Remove from pan.

Heat remaining 1 tablespoon oil in pan. Add peas; stir-fry for 1 minute. Add broth, soy, oyster sauce, and sugar; bring to a boil and cook for 1 minute. Combine cornstarch and water; add to pan. Cook, stirring, until sauce boils and thickens. Return squid to pan, stir, and serve at once. Makes 3 or 4 servings.

Szechwan Shrimp

Cooked in their shells, these spicy shrimp are incredibly tender. Because you cut the shells open to devein the shrimp before cooking, they're easy to eat with chopsticks.

  1 **pound medium-size or large shrimp**
  1 **tablespoon salt**
    Cooking Sauce (recipe follows)
  2½ **tablespoons salad oil**
  3 **large cloves garlic, minced**
  1 **teaspoon minced fresh ginger**
  ¼ **teaspoon crushed red pepper**
  4 **green onions (including tops), thinly sliced**

Cut shrimp through back of shell with scissors and devein. Place shrimp in a bowl and sprinkle with salt. With your hands, rub salt into shrimp. Let stand for 15 minutes, then rinse well, drain, and pat dry with paper towels.

Prepare Cooking Sauce and set aside.

Heat a wok or wide frying pan over medium heat. When pan is hot, add 1½ tablespoons of the oil. When oil begins to heat, add shrimp and stir-fry until shells turn pink (3 to 4 minutes). Remove from pan.

Heat remaining 1 tablespoon oil in pan over medium heat. Add garlic, ginger, and pepper and stir-fry for 5 seconds. Return shrimp to pan, add onions, and stir once. Stir Cooking Sauce, pour into pan, and cook, stirring, until sauce boils and thickens. Makes 3 or 4 servings.

Cooking Sauce. In a bowl, combine 1 tablespoon *each* **Worcestershire** and **dry sherry,** 2 tablespoons **catsup,** ¼ cup **water,** 2 teaspoons **sugar,** ½ teaspoon **salt,** and 1½ teaspoons **cornstarch.**

Chicken with Black Bean Sauce *(Recipe on facing page)* *with Steamed Rice (page 21)*

1 Add black beans and garlic to hot oil in wok; after just one stir, they'll be cooked.

2 Add bite-size pieces of marinated chicken to wok. Stir and toss constantly so pieces cook evenly; remove when opaque.

3 Using same stir-and-toss motion, cook vegetables until tender-crisp to bite.

4 Pour cooking sauce around edges of wok so it heats and cooks quickly. Cook until sauce bubbles and thickens.

 **Poultry**

Chicken with Black Bean Sauce

(Pictured on facing page)

Tender chicken and vegetables team up in a stir-fry from Canton. Vary the vegetable to suit your taste and the season; juicy bell peppers and fresh asparagus are two delicious choices.

- 1 teaspoon *each* cornstarch and soy sauce
- 2 teaspoons dry sherry
- 1 teaspoon water
- 1 whole chicken breast (about 1 lb.), skinned, boned, and cut into bite-size pieces
- 3½ tablespoons salad oil
  Cooking Sauce (recipe follows)
- 1 pound red or green bell peppers, or asparagus
- 2 teaspoons fermented black beans, rinsed, drained, and finely chopped
- 1 large clove garlic, minced
- 1 medium-size onion, cut into wedges, layers separated
- 1 tablespoon water

In a bowl, combine cornstarch, soy, sherry, and the 1 teaspoon water. Add chicken and stir to coat; then stir in 1½ teaspoons of the oil and let marinate for 15 minutes.

Prepare Cooking Sauce and set aside. Cut peppers into 1-inch-square pieces (or snap off and discard tough ends of asparagus; cut stalks diagonally into ½-inch slices).

Heat a wok or wide frying pan over high heat. When pan is hot, add 2 tablespoons of the oil. When oil begins to heat, add beans and garlic; stir once. Add chicken and stir-fry until opaque (about 3 minutes). Remove from pan.

Add remaining 1 tablespoon oil to pan. When oil is hot, add peppers and onion and stir-fry for 30 seconds. Add the 1 tablespoon water and cook, uncovered, until vegetables are tender-crisp to bite (about 1 minute). (If using asparagus, increase water to 2 tablespoons; cook, covered, for 2 minutes.) Return chicken to pan. Stir Cooking Sauce, pour into pan, and cook, stirring, until sauce boils and thickens. Makes 3 or 4 servings.

Cooking Sauce. In a small bowl, combine 1 tablespoon *each* **soy sauce** and **cornstarch,** ¼ teaspoon **sugar,** and ½ cup **regular-strength chicken broth** or water.

Cantonese Chicken & Vegetables

Crisp edible-pod peas add color and crunch to this savory stir-fry of chicken breast and mushrooms. A Cantonese cooking sauce, stirred in at the last minute, blends the flavors beautifully.

- 4 medium-size Oriental dried mushrooms
- 2 teaspoons *each* soy sauce, cornstarch, dry sherry, and water
  Dash of white pepper
- 1½ pounds chicken breasts, skinned, boned, and cut into bite-size pieces
- 3½ tablespoons salad oil
  Cooking Sauce (recipe follows)
- 1 small clove garlic, minced
- ½ cup sliced bamboo shoots
- ¼ pound edible-pod peas, ends and strings removed

Soak mushrooms in warm water to cover for 30 minutes; drain. Cut off and discard stems. Squeeze caps dry; slice thinly and set aside.

In a bowl, combine soy, cornstarch, sherry, water, and pepper. Add chicken and toss to coat; then stir in 1½ teaspoons of the oil and let marinate for about 15 minutes. Prepare Cooking Sauce and set aside.

Place a wok or wide frying pan over high heat. When pan is hot, add 2 tablespoons of the oil. When oil begins to heat, add garlic and stir once. Add chicken and stir-fry until opaque (about 3 minutes). Remove from pan.

Add remaining 1 tablespoon oil to pan. When oil is hot, add mushrooms and bamboo shoots. Stir-fry for 1 minute, adding a few drops of water if pan appears dry. Add peas and stir-fry for 1½ minutes, adding a few drops more water if pan appears dry. Return chicken to pan. Stir Cooking Sauce, pour into pan, and cook, stirring, until sauce boils and thickens. Makes 3 or 4 servings.

Cooking Sauce. In a small bowl, stir together ½ cup **water,** 1 tablespoon **dry sherry,** 2 tablespoons **oyster sauce** or soy sauce, ¼ teaspoon **sugar,** 1 teaspoon **sesame oil,** and 1 tablespoon **cornstarch.**

(Continued on next page)

Chinese Ways with Noodles

Fresh and dried Chinese noodles are available in Oriental markets and well-stocked supermarkets. If you find fresh noodles, you may want to buy several packages (they freeze well). Dried thin noodles and spaghetti are both good substitutes.

Try crisp wedges of Noodle Pancake as a base for stir-fries; offer Cold-stirred Noodles as a warm-weather lunch or supper entrée.

Chinese Noodles

- 16 **cups water**
- 1 **pound fresh or dried Chinese noodles**
- ½ **cup cold water**
- 1 **tablespoon sesame oil or salad oil**
- 1 **tablespoon soy sauce or ½ teaspoon salt**

Pour the 16 cups water into a large kettle and bring to a boil over high heat. Drop in noodles; stir to separate strands. When water returns to a boil, add the ½ cup cold water. Bring to a boil; boil until noodles are tender to bite (about 3 minutes for fresh noodles, 7 to 9 minutes for dried). Drain, rinse with cold water, and drain again. Stir in oil and soy. Serve immediately; or let cool, then cover and refrigerate for up to 2 days. Reheat by dipping in hot water. Makes about 4 servings.

Cold-stirred Noodles

Prepare **Chinese Noodles;** cover and refrigerate until cold. Divide cold noodles among 4 to 6 individual bowls and top with sliced **Barbecued Pork** (page 16) or cooked ham; blanched and chilled **bean sprouts;** and thinly sliced **cucumber, radishes,** and **green onions** (including tops). Let each diner season noodles to taste with **soy sauce, vinegar, sesame oil,** and **chili oil.** Makes 4 to 6 servings.

Noodle Pancake

Follow directions for **Chinese Noodles,** but use only ¾ pound noodles. Omit soy sauce; increase sesame oil to 2 tablespoons.

Place a 12-inch pizza pan or 10 by 15-inch rimmed baking sheet in a 500° oven. When pan is very hot, pour in 2 tablespoons **salad oil;** tilt to coat bottom and sides. Spread noodles evenly in pan and place on bottom rack of oven. Bake, uncovered, for 20 to 25 minutes or until golden on top and bottom. Cut into 4 to 6 equal portions. Makes 4 to 6 servings.

Cashew or Almond Chicken

In a wide frying pan or wok over medium-low heat, toast ½ cup **cashews** or blanched whole almonds in 1 tablespoon **salad oil** until golden; remove from pan and set aside. Then prepare **Cantonese Chicken & Vegetables;** stir in cashews just before serving.

Kung Pao Chicken

Charred dried chiles lend their breathtaking fire to mild morsels of chicken in this searing Szechwan specialty (it's one of the region's most popular culinary exports). In China, the chiles are eaten as part of the dish; if you don't enjoy fiery-hot food, you may prefer to discard them after charring.

Watch the chiles closely as they cook. If they burn, they'll release potent volatile oils that sting the nose and eyes.

- 1 **tablespoon** *each* **dry sherry and cornstarch**
- ½ **teaspoon salt**
- ⅛ **teaspoon white pepper**
- 1½ **pounds chicken breasts, skinned, boned, and cut into bite-size pieces**
- 4 **tablespoons salad oil**
  Cooking Sauce (recipe follows)
- 4 **to 6 small dried whole hot red chiles**
- ½ **cup salted peanuts**
- 1 **teaspoon** *each* **minced garlic and grated fresh ginger**
- 2 **green onions (including tops), cut into 1½-inch lengths**

In a bowl, combine sherry, cornstarch, salt, and pepper. Add chicken and stir to coat, then stir in 1 tablespoon of the oil and let marinate for 15 minutes. Prepare Cooking Sauce and set aside.

Heat a wok or wide frying pan over medium heat. When pan is hot, add 1 tablespoon of the oil. Add chiles and peanuts and cook, stirring, until chiles just begin to char. (If chiles become completely black, discard them. Remove peanuts from pan and set aside; repeat with new oil and chiles.) Remove peanuts and chiles from pan; set aside.

Pour remaining 2 tablespoons oil into pan and increase heat to high. When oil begins to heat, add garlic and ginger. Stir once, then add chicken. Stir-fry until chicken is opaque (about 3 minutes); add peanuts, chiles, and onions. Stir Cooking Sauce and pour into pan; cook, stirring, until sauce boils and thickens. Makes 4 servings.

Cooking Sauce. In a bowl, combine 2 tablespoons **soy sauce,** 1 tablespoon *each* **white wine vinegar** and **dry sherry,** 3 tablespoons **regular-strength chicken broth** or water, and 2 tablespoons *each* **sugar** and **cornstarch.**

Kung Pao Shrimp

Follow directions for **Kung Pao Chicken,** but substitute 1½ pounds **medium-size shrimp,** shelled and deveined, for chicken. Stir-fry shrimp until they turn pink (about 2 minutes).

Red-cooked Chicken

One easy-to-master Chinese cooking technique is "red cooking"—braising or stewing meat in a soy-based liquid that imparts a brownish-red color to the cooked food. If you wish, follow the example of Chinese cooks and re-use the braising liquid several times: just strain the leftover sauce, then refrigerate or freeze it until you prepare another red-cooked dish.

- 3 **tablespoons salad oil**
- 1 **frying chicken (3 to 3½ lbs.)**
- 1 **cup** *each* **soy sauce and water**
- ¼ **cup dry sherry**
- 3 **tablespoons sugar**
- 6 **slices fresh ginger,** *each* **⅛ by 1 by 3 inches**
- 2 **cloves garlic, minced or pressed**
- 3 **green onions (including tops), cut into 2-inch lengths**
  Fresh coriander (cilantro) sprigs
- ½ **cup water**

Heat oil in a wok or 5-quart kettle over medium-high heat. Add chicken and cook, turning frequently, until browned on all sides (15 to 20 minutes). Spoon off and discard fat. Add soy, the 1 cup water, sherry, sugar, ginger, garlic, and onions. Bring to a boil; then cover, reduce heat, and simmer, turning occasionally, until meat near thighbone is no longer pink when slashed (50 to 55 minutes). Lift chicken from sauce and place on a platter; let rest for about 10 minutes. Carve chicken and garnish with coriander.

Skim and discard fat from sauce. Measure out ½ cup sauce and pour into a small pan; strain remaining sauce and reserve for another time, if desired. Add the ½ cup water to sauce in pan and bring to a boil over medium-high heat.

Remove sauce from heat and place in a small bowl; pass at the table to spoon over individual servings. Makes 3 to 4 servings.

Coriander Chicken Salad

Hot, pungent, spicy-sweet, nutty—all describe *so see gai,* an out-of-the-ordinary chicken salad. The secret of the intriguing flavor combination is a special dressing, made with mustard, fresh coriander, five-spice and sesame. For a refreshing contrast of textures and flavors, serve the zesty chicken mixture on a bed of crisp shredded lettuce.

- 1 **frying chicken (3 to 3½ lbs.)**
- 2 **tablespoons soy sauce**
  Mustard Dressing (recipe follows)
- ¼ **cup sesame seeds**
- 5 **to 6 cups shredded iceberg lettuce**
- ¼ **cup** *each* **chopped fresh coriander (cilantro) and sliced green onions (including tops)**

Rinse chicken and pat dry. Place soy in a deep bowl; add chicken and turn to coat. Cover and refrigerate, turning often, for at least 2 hours or until next day. Lift chicken from bowl and place, breast side up, on a rack in a roasting pan. Roast in a 425° oven until skin is crisp and brown and meat near thighbone is no longer pink when slashed (about 45 minutes). Let cool on rack. Strip meat, with skin attached, from bones; cut into ¼-inch slivers. (At this point, you may cover and refrigerate until next day.)

Prepare Mustard Dressing and set aside. In a wide frying pan over medium heat, toast sesame seeds, shaking pan frequently, until golden (about 2 minutes).

Shortly before serving, arrange lettuce in a ½-inch-thick bed on a large platter. Combine chicken, coriander, onions, sesame seeds, and Mustard Dressing. Mix by lifting with 2 forks until blended. Mound chicken in center of lettuce. Makes about 4 servings.

Mustard Dressing. In a bowl, blend 1 tablespoon *each* **dry mustard** and **water;** then stir in ¼ cup *each* **sesame oil** and **salad oil,** 2 tablespoons **lemon juice,** 4 teaspoons *each* **sugar** and **soy sauce,** and 1 teaspoon **Chinese five-spice** or ½ teaspoon ground cinnamon. Stir until smooth. If made ahead, cover and let stand at room temperature until next day.

Tea-smoked Duck

(Pictured on facing page)

Traditional Szechwan tea-smoked duck is made in three steps: the duck is first smoked over tea leaves, then steamed, then deep-fried. We've simplified the process by eliminating the steaming step and substituting roasting for deep-frying.

> Plain Steamed Buns (recipe follows)
> 1 **duckling (about 4 lbs.)**
> 1 **teaspoon salt**
> 1 **tablespoon Szechwan peppercorns**
> 2 **tablespoons dry sherry**
> ¼ **cup** *each* **rice, firmly packed brown sugar, and black tea leaves**
> 2 **tablespoons coarsely chopped orange peel or dried tangerine peel**
> 6 **quarter-size slices fresh ginger, crushed**
> 5 **green onions (including tops)**
> **Hoisin sauce**
> **Fresh coriander (cilantro) sprigs**

Prepare Plain Steamed Buns and set aside. Remove giblets and neck from duck; reserve for other uses, if desired. Rinse duck inside and out and pat dry. Trim off and discard excess neck skin; with a fork, pierce remaining skin all over.

In a small frying pan over medium-low heat, cook salt and peppercorns, shaking pan often, until salt begins to brown and peppercorns become fragrant (about 10 minutes). Let cool, then coarsely grind with a mortar and pestle or crush with a rolling pin. Combine mixture with sherry; rub over duck, inside and out.

To smoke duck, you'll need a wok at least 14 inches in diameter (do not use an electric wok with a nonstick finish). Line wok with heavy-duty foil. Add rice, sugar, tea leaves, and orange peel; stir together. Position a round cake rack or steamer rack in bottom of wok, at least an inch above tea mixture. Set duck on rack; place wok over high heat.

When mixture begins to smoke, cover pan tightly and smoke for 5 minutes. Reduce heat to medium and continue to smoke, without uncovering wok, for 15 minutes. Turn off heat and leave covered until smoke subsides (about 15 more minutes). Remove duck. (At this point, you may cover and refrigerate until next day.) Discard tea mixture. Place ginger and 2 of the onions inside duck cavity; fasten opening shut with a small skewer, if necessary. Place duck, breast side down, on a rack in a roasting pan. Bake in a 350° oven for 1½ hours. Drain and discard fat from pan and turn duck over; continue to bake for 45 minutes to 1 hour or until thigh feels soft when pressed. Remove duck from oven; drain and discard all fat from pan. Increase oven temperature to 450°; return duck to oven and cook for about 5 minutes or just until skin is crisp.

Slice duck meat from bones; cut remaining 3 onions into thin slivers. Steam buns for 5 minutes to reheat. Place duck slices in a warm bun; top with onions, hoisin, and coriander, then close and eat out of hand. Makes 2 or 3 servings.

Plain Steamed Buns. Prepare dough as for **Pork-filled Buns** (page 17); omit filling. Shape dough into 12 round buns and place each on a 3-inch square of foil. Let rise for 30 minutes; steam for 12 to 15 minutes.

Duck with Noodles

Ready-cooked ducks from a Chinese delicatessen or meat market may seem like an extravagance—but in fact, they usually cost little more than raw duck. If you have to make a special trip to find them, buy several; they freeze well.

> Noodle Pancake (page 28)
> 1 **Chinese barbecued duck (about 2½ lbs.)**
> **Duck juices (usually sold with duck) or regular-strength chicken broth**
> 1 *each* **small green and red bell pepper (or 2 small green peppers), cut into thin strips**
> 1 **small head napa cabbage (about ¾ lb.), cut crosswise into 1-inch slices**

Prepare Noodle Pancake and set aside.

Drain any liquid from inside duck and combine with duck juices. Measure; add broth, if necessary, to make ⅔ cup. (If duck did not come with packaged juices, you may use ⅔ cup broth.)

Pull duck meat, with skin attached, from bones. Cut meat and skin into 1-inch chunks; set aside.

Pour juices into a wide frying pan; bring to a boil over high heat. Add duck and peppers; then cover, reduce heat to medium-high, and simmer until duck and peppers are warm (about 4 minutes). Lift duck and peppers from juices; set aside and keep warm. Stir cabbage into hot juices; cover and cook until slices from stem end are tender to bite (about 5 minutes).

To serve, spoon duck and peppers over wedges of Noodle Pancake; spoon cabbage alongside. Makes 4 servings.

Tea-smoked Duck *with Plain Steamed Buns* (Recipes on facing page)

1 Toast peppercorns and salt until peppercorns become fragrant and salt begins to brown. Shake pan often while cooking.

2 Grind peppercorn mixture with a mortar and pestle (or crush with rolling pin); mix with dry sherry.

3 Rub duck, inside and out, with spicy peppercorn and sherry mixture.

4 After smoking over fragrant blend of sugar, tea, and orange peel, duck is ready for roasting.

 # Meats

Mongolian Grill

The Mongols introduced the Chinese to lamb—and to the dome-shaped grill on which it's often cooked. You can use an electric griddle or frying pan in place of the grill for this cook-at-the-table meal of lamb and vegetables.

- 12 Mandarin Pancakes (page 35), or Steamed Rice (page 21)
  Seasoning Sauces (recipes follow)
- 3 pounds lamb shoulder chops or 2 pounds lean boneless beef (sirloin or top round)
- 3 large carrots, shredded
- 2 large onions, thinly sliced
- ¾ pound bean sprouts
- 2 green peppers, cut into ¼-inch strips
- 3 cups shredded cabbage
  Salad oil

Prepare Mandarin Pancakes and set aside. Prepare sauces; pour into separate bowls.

Cut lamb from bones. Trim and discard fat; then slice meat across the grain into strips ¼ inch thick and 2 to 3 inches long. Place meat, carrots, onions, sprouts, peppers, and cabbage in separate bowls.

At serving time, heat pancakes as directed on page 35. Preheat an electric griddle to 350°. For each serving, have each diner select several slices of meat and about 1 cup of vegetables, then mix vegetables with 1 to 2 tablespoons of seasoning sauces.

Servings are cooked individually. For each serving, brush griddle with about 1 teaspoon oil and put on meat. Cook meat, turning, until lightly browned (about 1 minute); add vegetables. Continue to cook and stir meat and vegetables until vegetables are tender (about 1 minute). Spoon filling into pancakes, wrap up, and eat out of hand (or serve with rice). Makes about 2 servings for each of 6 diners.

Hot Chili Sauce. In a small bowl, combine 1 teaspoon **chili oil** or 1½ teaspoons liquid hot pepper seasoning with ¾ cup **soy sauce.**

Garlic Sauce. Place 1½ teaspoons **minced garlic** and 1 teaspoon **salt** in a mortar and pestle; crush into a smooth paste. Add ⅓ cup **white wine vinegar** and 2 tablespoons **water;** stir until well blended.

Lemon-Ginger Sauce. Grate 1 teaspoon yellow peel from 2 large **lemons;** set aside. Remove and discard remaining peel and all white membrane; slice lemons thinly and remove seeds. Place lemon slices in a blender or food processor. Add grated peel, one 1-inch piece peeled **fresh ginger,** thinly sliced, and ¼ cup **water.** Whirl until smooth.

Sweet & Sour Pork

Tender meat, juicy pineapple, ruby red sauce—it's no wonder that this Cantonese standard is so popular with diners.

- ½ to 1 pound lean boneless pork (butt or leg), cut into 1-inch cubes
- 1 cup water
- 1 quarter-size slice fresh ginger
- 1 tablespoon soy sauce
  Sweet-Sour Sauce (recipe follows)
- 1 egg
- ½ cup cornstarch
  About 4 tablespoons salad oil
- 1 medium-size onion, cut into wedges, layers separated
- 1 green pepper, cut into 1-inch squares
- 1 clove garlic, minced
- 2 small tomatoes, cut into wedges
- ½ cup canned pineapple chunks, drained

Place pork, water, ginger, and soy in a 2 to 3-quart pan; bring to a boil over high heat. Cover, reduce heat, and simmer for 5 minutes. Drain and let cool. Prepare Sweet-Sour Sauce and set aside.

Beat egg in a small bowl. Place cornstarch in a plastic bag. Dip pork cubes in egg, then shake in cornstarch until lightly coated; shake off excess. Heat about 2 tablespoons of the oil in a wok or wide frying pan over medium-high heat.

When oil is hot, add meat (cook half at a time if using more than ½ pound). Stir-fry until browned (2 to 3 minutes). Remove meat and set aside; discard pan drippings.

Increase heat to high and add remaining 2 tablespoons oil. When oil is hot, add onion, green pepper, and garlic and stir-fry for 1 minute, adding a few drops of water if pan appears dry. Stir Sweet-Sour Sauce, pour into pan, and cook, stirring, until sauce boils and thickens slightly.

Stir in tomatoes, pineapple, and pork and cook just until heated through (about 30 seconds). Makes 2 to 4 servings.

Sweet-Sour Sauce. In a bowl, combine ¾ cup **water**; 1 tablespoon *each* **cornstarch, catsup,** and **soy sauce**; ¼ cup *each* **sugar** and **wine vinegar**; and a few drops of **liquid hot pepper seasoning.**

Yu-shiang Pork

Yu-shiang pork is often called fish-flavored pork—not because it contains fish, but because its seasoning is so typical of Szechwan fish cookery.

- 1 teaspoon cornstarch
- ¼ teaspoon salt
  Dash of white pepper
- 1 tablespoon dry sherry
- ¾ pound lean boneless pork (butt or leg), cut into matchstick pieces
- 3½ tablespoons salad oil
  Cooking Sauce (recipe follows)
- 2 cloves garlic, minced
- 1 teaspoon minced fresh ginger
- 3 or 4 small dried whole hot red chiles
- ⅔ cup sliced bamboo shoots, cut into matchstick pieces
- 10 green onions (including tops) cut into 2-inch lengths

Combine cornstarch, salt, pepper, and sherry. Add pork and 1½ teaspoons of the oil; stir to coat. Let marinate for 15 minutes. Prepare Cooking Sauce. Heat a wok or wide frying pan over high heat. When pan is hot, add 2 tablespoons of the oil. When oil begins to heat, add garlic, ginger, and chiles; stir once. Add pork and stir-fry until lightly browned (about 4 minutes); remove from pan.

Heat remaining 1 tablespoon oil in pan. Add bamboo shoots and onions and stir-fry for 1 minute. Return pork to pan. Stir Cooking Sauce, pour into pan, and cook, stirring, until sauce boils and thickens. Makes 4 servings.

Cooking Sauce. In a bowl, combine 1 tablespoon *each* **sugar, vinegar,** and **dry sherry**; 2 tablespoons **soy sauce**; 3 tablespoons **regular-strength chicken broth** or water; and 2 teaspoons **cornstarch.**

Yu-shiang Lamb

Follow directions for **Yu-shiang Pork,** but substitute about 1¼ pounds **lamb shoulder** or loin chops for pork. Cut meat off bones; trim and discard fat, then cut meat into matchstick pieces.

Mu Shu Pork

(Pictured on page 34)

Pancakes, steamed buns, and noodles are common fare in northern China, where wheat is grown more extensively than rice. The thin pancakes are often used as wrappers for savory meat mixtures—as here, where they're filled with pork, vegetables, and spicy hoisin sauce.

- About 18 Mandarin Pancakes (recipe follows)
  Green onion brushes (directions follow)
- ⅓ cup dried tiger lily buds
- 4 dried black fungus (also called cloud or tree ears)
- 1 teaspoon cornstarch
- 1 tablespoon *each* soy sauce and dry sherry
- ½ pound lean boneless pork (butt or leg), cut into matchstick pieces
- 3½ tablespoons salad oil
  Cooking Sauce (recipe follows)
- 5 green onions (including tops)
- 4 eggs
- ¼ teaspoon salt
- ½ teaspoon minced fresh ginger
- ½ cup sliced bamboo shoots, cut into matchstick pieces
- 1 small carrot, shredded
- 2 cups shredded iceberg lettuce
  Hoisin sauce

Prepare Mandarin Pancakes and set aside. Also prepare green onion brushes.

Soak lily buds and fungus in warm water to cover for 30 minutes; drain. Pinch off and discard hard tips of lily buds; cut buds in half lengthwise. Pinch out and discard hard, knobby centers of fungus; thinly slice remaining fungus.

In a bowl, combine cornstarch, soy, and sherry. Add pork and stir to coat. Stir in 1½ teaspoons of the oil. Let marinate for 15 minutes. Prepare Cooking Sauce and set aside.

Cut onions into 1½-inch lengths; then cut lengthwise into thin shreds. Reserve half the onion shreds for cooking; set other half aside to pass at the table.

In a bowl, lightly beat eggs with salt. Heat a wok or wide frying pan over medium-high heat. When pan is hot, add 1 tablespoon of the oil. When oil is hot, add eggs and cook, stirring, until softly set; then turn out of pan.

Pour remaining 2 tablespoons oil into pan and increase heat to high. When oil begins to heat, add

(Continued on page 35)

Mandarin Pancakes with Mu Shu Pork *(Recipes on page 33 and facing page)*

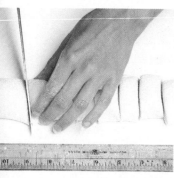

1 With your hands, roll dough into a 12-inch-long log; cut into 12 equal pieces. Then cut each piece in half, making 24 pieces total.

2 Shape each piece into small flat round. Brush one round with sesame oil; then top with a second round and press lightly to sandwich rounds together.

3 Roll 2-layer round to a 7 to 8-inch circle; cook in an ungreased frying pan, turning every 15 seconds, until pancake puffs and turns parchment color.

4 Carefully pull sections apart to make two paper-thin pancakes. Serve with Mu Shu Pork.

ginger and stir once. Add pork and stir-fry until lightly browned (about 4 minutes). Add lily buds and fungus and stir-fry for 1 minute, adding a few drops of water if pan appears dry. Add bamboo shoots, carrot, lettuce, reserved onion shreds, and Cooking Sauce; cook, stirring, just until lettuce is wilted (about 2 minutes). Stir in eggs, breaking them into bite-size pieces. When eggs are hot, pour mixture into a serving dish and serve at once.

Have on the table Mandarin Pancakes, hoisin, onion shreds, and green onion brushes. To eat, paint a little hoisin on a pancake with a green onion brush, spoon on some of the meat mixture, and garnish with onion shreds. Wrap to enclose filling and eat out of hand. Makes 4 to 6 servings.

Green onion brushes. Cut the white part of 3 **green onions** into 1½-inch lengths. Using scissors or a sharp knife, slash each end of onion pieces lengthwise 3 or 4 times, ½ inch into onion. Cover with **ice water;** refrigerate until ends curl (about 1 hour).

Cooking Sauce. In a bowl, combine 1 tablespoon *each* **soy sauce, dry sherry,** and **water;** 1 teaspoon *each* **sugar, cornstarch,** and **sesame oil;** and ¼ teaspoon **salt.**

Mandarin Pancakes. Place 2 cups **all-purpose flour** in a bowl. With a fork or chopsticks, mix in ¾ cup **boiling water.** Stir dough until it holds together; then turn out onto a lightly floured board and knead until smooth and satiny (about 10 minutes). Cover and let rest at room temperature for 30 minutes. Roll dough into a 12-inch-long log. Cut into 12 equal pieces and keep covered.

You can make 2 pancakes from each piece of dough. First, cut 1 piece of dough exactly in half. Roll each half into a ball and flatten slightly. Roll each ball on a lightly floured board to a round 3 inches in diameter. Brush top of one round lightly with **sesame oil** or salad oil (you'll need about 2 tablespoons *total*). Cover oil-coated round with the other round. Press the 2 rounds lightly but firmly together. Place the double round on a lightly floured board and roll out from center to edges until 7 to 8 inches in diameter. Turn frequently; brush board lightly with flour as necessary. Repeat with 1 or 2 more pieces of dough, to make a total of 2 or 3 two-layer pancakes; cook these before rolling more.

Heat an ungreased wide frying pan over medium heat; place 1 two-layer pancake in pan. Turn pancake about every 15 seconds until it's blistered by air pockets, turns parchment color, and feels dry. Pancake should not be brown, but a few golden spots won't hurt. (Pancake becomes brittle if overcooked.) Remove from pan. Carefully pull the 2 halves apart. Stack on a plate and keep covered. Cook remaining 2-layer cakes, pull apart, and add to stack. Repeat rolling, cooking, and stacking until all pancakes have been prepared. Serve warm; or let cool, wrap airtight, and refrigerate or freeze for later use.

To reheat, thaw if frozen. Line a flat-bottomed steamer with a towel dipped in water and wrung dry; stack pancakes inside and fold towel over them. Cover and steam for 5 minutes. Fold hot pancakes in half, then in half again. Since they dry out quickly, serve just a few at a time and keep remainder covered. Makes 24 pancakes.

Beef with Snow Peas

Marinated beef and edible-pod peas (often called snow peas) combine in this spicy stir-fry. The dish owes its complex flavors to the marinade.

> 1 **pound lean boneless beef (sirloin or top round)**
> **Marinade (recipe follows)**
> ¾ **pound edible-pod peas, ends and strings removed**
> 1 **tablespoon water**
> 4 **tablespoons salad oil**
> 1 **tablespoon soy sauce**
> 1 **teaspoon sugar**
> 1 **small onion, cut into slivers**

Trim and discard fat from beef; cut meat into 1-inch chunks. With a mallet, pound each piece to a thickness of about ¼ inch. Prepare Marinade; stir in beef, then cover and refrigerate for at least 2 hours or until next day.

Heat a wok or wide frying pan over high heat. When pan is hot, add peas, water, and 2 tablespoons of the oil; stir-fry until peas are tender (2 to 3 minutes). Transfer to a serving dish. Return pan to heat and add remaining 2 tablespoons oil; when oil is hot, add beef mixture. Stir-fry until meat is lightly browned (about 2 minutes). Stir together soy and sugar; add to pan along with onion. Cook for 1 more minute. Makes about 4 servings.

Marinade. In a bowl, combine 2 tablespoons **salad oil** and 1 tablespoon *each* **soy sauce, catsup, dry sherry, cornstarch, hoisin sauce,** and **sesame oil.** If desired, stir in 1 tablespoon **Tientsin preserved vegetables;** then add 1 teaspoon **Worcestershire** and 1 clove **garlic,** minced or pressed.

# Vegetables

Stir-fried Vegetables

Bright color, delightful tender-crisp texture, and sweet natural flavor make stir-fried vegetables a welcome addition to any meal.

> Cooking Sauce (optional; recipe follows)
> Prepared vegetables (directions follow)
> 2 tablespoons salad oil
> ½ teaspoon minced fresh ginger
> 1 small clove garlic, minced
> ½ teaspoon *each* salt and sugar
> Regular-strength chicken broth or water

If you wish to serve your vegetables with sauce, prepare Cooking Sauce and set aside. Prepare vegetable of your choice; have ready beside pan.

Heat a wok or wide frying pan over high heat. When pan is hot, add oil. When oil begins to heat, add ginger and garlic; stir once. Add vegetable and stir-fry for 1 minute. Add salt, sugar, and indicated amount of broth; cover (if necessary) and cook until vegetable is tender-crisp to bite.

If you wish to serve a combination of vegetables with different textures, add firmest vegetable to pan first and partially cook; add more tender vegetables near end of cooking time. Or cook vegetables separately, then combine them for reheating.

Serve vegetables as is; or stir Cooking Sauce, pour into pan, and cook, stirring, until sauce boils and thickens (about 30 seconds). Makes 4 servings.

Cooking Sauce. In a bowl, combine ½ cup **regular-strength chicken broth** or water, 1 tablespoon **cornstarch,** and 2 teaspoons **soy sauce.**

Prepared vegetables. Choose one or more of the following; you'll need a total of 1 pound.

Asparagus. Cut diagonally into ¼-inch slices. Stir-fry for 1 minute. Add 2 tablespoons broth; cover and cook for 2 to 3 minutes.

Bean sprouts. Leave whole. Stir-fry for 1 minute. Add a few drops of broth and toss for 1 to 2 minutes.

Bok choy. Cut stems into ½-inch pieces; cut leaves into 2-inch pieces. Stir-fry stems for 1 minute. Add leaves and stir-fry for 30 seconds. Add 1 tablespoon broth; cover and cook for 2 to 3 minutes.

Broccoli. Cut off flowerets; slash their stems. Peel stalks; slice thinly. Stir-fry for 1 minute. Add 2 tablespoons broth; cover and cook for 3 to 4 minutes.

Cabbage (all varieties). Cut into ¼-inch slices or 1-inch pieces. Stir-fry for 1 minute. Add 1 tablespoon broth; cover and cook for 2 minutes.

Carrots. Cut diagonally into ¼-inch slices. Stir-fry for 1 minute. Add 3 tablespoons broth; cover and cook for 3 to 4 minutes.

Edible-pod peas. Break off ends and remove strings. Stir-fry for 1 minute. (No broth or covered cooking time is required.)

Green beans. Cut into 1-inch pieces. Stir-fry for 1 minute. Add 3 tablespoons broth; cover and cook for 4 minutes.

Mushrooms (fresh). Cut lengthwise into ¼-inch slices. Stir-fry for 1 minute. Add 1 tablespoon broth and toss for 2 minutes.

Onions. Cut into slices; or cut into wedges and separate layers. Stir-fry for 1 to 2 minutes. (No broth or covered cooking time is required.)

Peppers (red or green bell). Cut into 1-inch pieces or ¼-inch slices. Stir-fry for 1 minute. Add 1 tablespoon broth and toss for 1 minute.

Zucchini (and all summer squash varieties). Cut into ¼-inch slices. Stir-fry for 1 minute. Add 1 tablespoon broth; cover and cook for 3 minutes.

Marinated Lotus Root
(Pictured on front cover)

Crisp fresh lotus root, available at Oriental markets, stars in this refreshing salad (don't substitute canned lotus root for fresh). You can use carrots or edible-pod peas in place of lotus root.

> 1 pound fresh lotus root
> 1 tablespoon *each* soy sauce and white (distilled) vinegar
> 2 teaspoons sugar
> ¼ teaspoon salt
> 1 teaspoon sesame oil

Peel lotus root. Cut off and discard ends; cut root into ⅛-inch slices. Drop slices into a bowl of cold water to prevent discoloration. Bring a pan of water to boiling. Drain lotus root; then drop into pan and cook until tender-crisp to bite (about 3 minutes). Drain, rinse with cold water, and drain again.

Place soy, vinegar, sugar, salt, and oil in a plastic bag; add lotus root. Seal bag and refrigerate, turning occasionally to distribute marinade, for at least 1 hour or up to 8 hours. Makes 8 servings.

Carrots. Cut 1 pound **carrots** into ⅛-inch slices. Increase cooking time to 4 minutes.

Edible-pod peas. Remove strings from ½ pound **edible-pod peas.** Cook for only 30 seconds.

Szechwan Eggplant

Braised in a hot, savory broth, eggplant turns out soft and tender. A small amount of pork adds rich, meaty flavor to the sauce.

    ½ cup regular-strength chicken broth
    1 teaspoon *each* sugar and vinegar
    1 tablespoon soy sauce
    ½ teaspoon salt
      Dash of pepper
    1 large eggplant or about 3 Oriental eggplant
      (about 1¼ pounds *total*)
    5 tablespoons salad oil
    ¼ pound ground pork
    2 green onions (including tops), finely chopped
    1 teaspoon minced fresh ginger
    2 teaspoons minced garlic
    2 teaspoons hot bean sauce or 2 small dried
      whole hot red chiles (crumbled and seeded,
      if desired)
    1 teaspoon cornstarch
    1 tablespoon water
    1 teaspoon sesame oil

In a bowl, combine broth, sugar, vinegar, soy, salt, and pepper; set aside. Peel eggplant, if desired (don't peel Oriental eggplant); cut into strips 2 inches long and ½ inch thick.

Heat a wok or wide frying pan over medium-high heat. When pan is hot, add 3 tablespoons of the salad oil. When oil is hot, add eggplant and stir-fry for 3 minutes. (Eggplant will soak up oil immediately; stir continuously to prevent burning.) Remove from pan.

Heat remaining 2 tablespoons salad oil in pan. Add pork, onions, ginger, garlic, and bean sauce. Stir-fry until meat is no longer pink (about 2 minutes). Return eggplant to pan and pour in broth mixture; cover and cook over medium-low heat until eggplant is tender when pierced (about 6 minutes).

In a cup, stir together cornstarch and water. Pour into pan and cook, stirring, until sauce boils and thickens. Stir in sesame oil. Makes 4 servings.

Sprout & Cress Salad

This chilly tangle of bean sprouts and peppery watercress makes a refreshing break between courses; it's a good cold appetizer, too.

    ¾ pound bean sprouts
    1 bunch watercress
    2 tablespoons soy sauce
    1 tablespoon *each* vinegar and sesame oil
    1 teaspoon sugar

Half-fill a 5 to 6-quart kettle with water. Bring to a boil over high heat. Drop in bean sprouts and cook for 30 seconds. Drain, rinse with cold water, and drain again. Cover and refrigerate until cold.

Discard tough stems from watercress; then tear into 2-inch lengths. Stir together soy, vinegar, oil, and sugar. Drain bean sprouts again; combine with watercress and dressing. Toss until vegetables are well coated. Makes 4 servings.

Eight Immortal Jai

Bot bo jai is a traditional Cantonese vegetarian dish of crisp and colorful vegetables in a delicate sauce.

    ½ cup (¾ oz.) dried black fungus (also called
      cloud or tree ears)
    1 tablespoon *each* cornstarch and water
    1 cup regular-strength chicken broth
    1 tablespoon soy sauce
    2 tablespoons salad oil
    ½ teaspoon minced fresh ginger
    1 small clove garlic, minced or pressed
    1½ cups *each* broccoli flowerets and thinly
      sliced carrots
    1 can (2¼ oz.) sliced water chestnuts, drained

Soak fungus in warm water to cover for 30 minutes; drain. Pinch out and discard hard, knobby centers; cut remaining fungus into bite-size pieces.

In a small bowl, blend cornstarch and water; stir in broth and soy and set aside.

Heat oil in a wok or wide frying pan over high heat. Add ginger, garlic, broccoli, carrots, and fungus. Stir-fry for 1 minute. Stir cornstarch mixture to blend; add to vegetables along with water chestnuts. Cook, stirring, until sauce boils, thickens, and turns clear. Makes 4 to 6 servings.

 # Desserts

Caramel Fried Apples or Bananas

(Pictured on facing page)

This show-stopper of a dessert is hardly a typical ending to a Chinese meal—but it's always popular with diners. Caramelizing the sugar calls for split-second timing; it goes so quickly that you don't have time to use a candy thermometer. You may want to practice this step once before making the whole dessert.

> ½ cup all-purpose flour
> 2 tablespoons cornstarch
> ¾ teaspoon baking powder
>   Water
> 2 golden Delicious apples or 2 bananas
>   Salad oil
>   Ice cubes
> ⅔ cup sugar
> 2 teaspoons sesame seeds

In a bowl, mix flour, cornstarch, and baking powder. Add ½ cup water and stir until smooth. Peel and core apples; cut each into 8 wedges. (If you use bananas, peel, then cut diagonally into ½-inch slices.) Place fruit in batter and turn to coat evenly.

Into a deep, heavy pan (about 6 inches in diameter), pour oil to a depth of about 1½ inches and heat to 350° on a deep-frying thermometer. Using chopsticks or a spoon, lift fruit, 1 piece at a time, from batter. Let excess drip off; then lower fruit into hot oil (cook several pieces at a time). Cook until coating is golden brown (about 2 minutes). Remove with a slotted spoon and drain on paper towels.

When all fruit has been cooked, generously oil a shallow pan or flat serving dish. Fill a serving bowl to the brim with ice cubes; add water to cover.

To make the caramel coating, place sugar, ⅓ cup warm water, and 1 tablespoon oil in a 10-inch frying pan; stir to blend. Place pan over high heat. When mixture begins to bubble (about 1 minute), shake pan continuously to prevent burning. Continue cooking and shaking pan until syrup *just* turns a pale straw color (about 9 minutes). Immediately remove from heat, add sesame seeds, and swirl to mix. (Syrup will continue to cook after you remove it from heat and will turn to a golden color in a few seconds.) Drop a few pieces of fruit into syrup and swirl to coat evenly. Using 2 spoons, immediately remove each piece of fruit; arrange on oiled pan (pieces should not touch). Repeat with remaining fruit. At the table, dip fruit in ice to harden coating and cool fruit. Makes 6 servings.

Almond Cookies

These rich and tender cookies are one of the very few traditional Chinese baked desserts. For variety, try topping them with sesame seeds.

> 1 cup (½ lb.) lard or solid shortening
> ½ cup granulated sugar
> ¼ cup firmly packed brown sugar
> 1 egg
> 1 teaspoon almond extract
> 2¼ cups unsifted all-purpose flour
> ⅛ teaspoon salt
> 1½ teaspoons baking powder
>   About 60 whole blanched almonds
> 1 egg yolk
> 2 tablespoons water

In a large bowl, cream lard, granulated sugar, and brown sugar until fluffy. Add egg and almond extract; beat until well blended. Sift flour with salt and baking powder. Add to creamed mixture; mix well.

To shape each cooky, roll 1 tablespoon of dough into a ball. Place balls 2 inches apart on ungreased baking sheets. Gently press down on each ball, making a 2-inch round. Press an almond in center of each round. In a small bowl, beat egg yolk with water; brush mixture over top of each cooky.

Bake in a 350° oven for 10 to 12 minutes or until lightly browned. Transfer cookies to wire racks and let cool completely. Store in an airtight container. Makes about 60 cookies.

Sesame Cookies

Follow directions for **Almond Cookies,** but substitute about ¼ cup **sesame seeds** for almonds. To shape each cooky, press a ball of dough between your palms to make a 2-inch round. Brush egg yolk mixture on one side of each round, then dip coated side in sesame seeds. Place cookies on baking sheets seeded side up.

Caramel Fried Apples *(Recipe on facing page)*

1 Deep-fry batter-coated apple wedges, several pieces at a time, until coating is golden brown.

2 Swirl and shake pan of bubbling syrup constantly to prevent burning.

3 Remove pan of caramel syrup from heat the instant it turns a pale straw color. Add sesame seeds and swirl to mix; then drop in fruit and swirl to coat.

4 Work quickly to transfer caramel-coated fruit to oiled dish or pan. At the table, dunk fruit in ice to harden coating.

The Cooking of
Japan

Freshness, simplicity, and elegance of presentation: these are the guiding principles of Japanese cooking, principles followed by good cooks the world around.

Well-prepared Japanese food always begins with the freshest possible ingredients: a strong sensitivity to the time of year has helped to shape a cuisine stressing dishes compatible with each season. There are succulent cucumbers in summer and shiitake mushrooms in autumn; warming soups take the chill off blustery winter days, and ice-cold noodle dishes temper summer's heat.

The principle of simplicity goes hand in hand with the stress on freshness. Ingredients are prepared simply and sauced with restraint; the aim is to enhance—not mask—each food's natural qualities. Elegant simplicity also guides presentation. Small portions of a few foods are gracefully arranged on the plate, in a carefully chosen composition of shapes and colors. The Japanese are masters at making simple foods beautiful; cut into flower-shaped slices, a common carrot can delight diners with its beauty as well as its taste.

Soups

Miso Soup

There is no more authentic beginning to a Japanese meal than a small bowl of miso soup. Look for miso, a fermented soybean paste, in Oriental markets. It's available in white and red (red miso is saltier).

Green onions and creamy tofu are typical Japanese garnishes for clear soups; a watercress sprig, a few thin carrot or mushroom slices, or small spinach leaves are other possibilities. Keep garnishes simple—and add them (as the Japanese do) with a light hand.

- 5 **cups dashi (basic soup stock—directions follow)**
- ¼ **cup white miso (fermented soybean paste)**
- ¼ **pound tofu (bean curd), drained and cut into strips about ½ by ½ inch**
- 1 **green onion (including top), cut into 1-inch-long julienne strips**

Place dashi, miso, and tofu in a 2 to 3-quart pan; bring to a boil over high heat. Ladle into small bowls; garnish with onion. Makes 6 servings.

Dashi. *Dashi* is made from dried bonito flakes (*katsuobushi*) and dried tangle seaweed (*kombu*), both available at Japanese markets. You don't have to make dashi from scratch, though. We recommend an excellent and convenient alternative: *dashi-no-moto*, instant dashi that's available in several forms. Prepare according to package directions. Regular-strength chicken broth (skimmed of fat) also makes an acceptable substitute for dashi, though the flavor isn't really authentic.

Miso Soup with Egg

Place 4 cups **dashi** and ¼ cup **white miso** in a 2 to 3-quart pan; bring to a boil over high heat. In a cup, lightly beat 1 **egg.** Swirling soup in pan, add egg very gradually, letting it trickle into pan (cooked egg will form thin, ribbonlike strands). Remove from heat. If desired, add 2 teaspoons **mirin** or cream sherry. Place a twist of **orange peel** or lemon peel in each of 4 to 6 small soup bowls; ladle in soup. Sprinkle with slices of **green onion** (including top). Makes 4 to 6 servings.

Japanese fisherman packs up his net and ropes after a productive trip; woven baskets hold the day's catch.

Rolled Sushi *(Recipe on facing page)* with Hand-shaped Sushi *(page 44)*

1 Draw sheet of nori back and forth over flame to toast it. You can toast nori several hours ahead of time.

2 With moistened fingers, pat rice all the way to side and bottom edges of nori, and to within 2 inches of top edge.

3 Hold filling (bluefin tuna and cucumber here) in place with your fingers; lift up mat with thumbs. Roll near edge of nori over to meet far edge of rice; press.

4 Slice down firmly through roll at 1-inch intervals to make bite-size pieces. (Do not cut with a sawing motion.)

Rice & Noodles

Rolled Sushi

(Pictured on facing page and on front cover)

For rolled (*maki*) sushi, you spread rice on a seaweed or egg wrapper, roll up, and cut into bite-size pieces. Hand-shaped (*nigiri*) sushi is molded into cakes or balls with the hands. You make hand-rolled (*temaki*) sushi a piece at a time, filling small seaweed squares with assorted ingredients. *Maki* and *nigiri* offer the advantage of portability; sushi is common picnic and lunchbox fare in Japan.

Rice for sushi is traditionally cooled by fanning with a hand-held fan, but you can simply let it stand at room temperature until cool.

> About 5 sheets roasted or unroasted nori; or Egg Wrappers (recipe follows); or some of each
>
> Sushi Rice (recipe follows)
>
> Prepared vegetables (directions follow)
>
> Wasabi paste (directions follow)
>
> ½ pound yellowfin or bluefin tuna, sea bass, halibut, Pacific snapper, or salmon, boned, skinned, and cut into ½ by ½ by 5-inch strips
>
> Soy sauce
>
> Pickled red ginger (*shoga*)

Toast nori by drawing it, 1 sheet at a time, back and forth over a low gas flame or an electric element set on low until crisp. Prepare Egg Wrappers (if used), Sushi Rice, vegetables, and wasabi paste. To assemble, place 1 sheet of nori or 1 Egg Wrapper on a *sudare* or a bamboo placemat with slats running parallel to you. Place about 1½ cups rice on nori (about 1 cup rice on an Egg Wrapper). With moistened hands, pat down rice to a thickness of about ½ inch, spreading it out to side and bottom edges of nori and to 2 inches below top edge. Arrange about 1 ounce fish and 1 or 2 kinds of vegetables in rows across middle of rice. Holding fish and vegetables down with your fingers, lift up mat with thumbs and roll over so that near edge of nori meets far edge of rice. Press mat around roll briefly; press in any loose ingredients at ends. Remove mat; cut roll into eight 1-inch slices. Repeat with remaining nori, rice, and fillings. Offer soy and wasabi paste for dipping; serve ginger alongside. Makes 30 to 40 pieces.

Egg Wrappers. In a bowl, combine 4 **eggs**, 1 teaspoon *each* **sugar** and **soy sauce**, and 4 teaspoons **sake**, dry sherry, or water. Place a pan (preferably one with a nonstick finish) measuring 8 inches across the bottom over medium-low heat. When pan is hot, brush with about ½ teaspoon **salad oil**. Using a ¼-cup measure, dip out about 3 tablespoons of the egg mixture. Pour into pan all at once; quickly tilt pan to coat bottom evenly. Cook just until egg is set and feels dry on top; turn out onto a plate lined with paper towels. Repeat with remaining egg mixture, brushing pan with oil each time; stack wrappers as you cook them. Trim edges to make rectangles about 6½ by 5½ inches. Makes 5 pancakes.

Sushi Rice. In a 3 to 4-quart pan, cover 3 cups **short-grain (pearl) rice** with water; stir, then drain. Repeat until water is clear; drain. Add 3½ cups **water** to drained rice. Cover and bring to a boil over high heat. Reduce heat to low; cook, without stirring, until all water is absorbed (about 15 minutes).

Gently stir in ⅓ cup **seasoned rice vinegar** for sushi (or ⅓ cup white (distilled) or white wine vinegar mixed with 2 tablespoons sugar and seasoned to taste with salt). Divide rice equally between 2 rimmed baking sheets; spread out. Let cool to room temperature. (If made ahead, cover and store at room temperature until next day. *Do not refrigerate.*)

Prepared vegetables. Choose 1 or 2 from the following:

Carrots. Cut 2 **carrots** into 3 to 4-inch-long julienne strips. Into a small pan, pour ⅓ cup **seasoned rice vinegar** for sushi (or alternate; see **Sushi Rice**). Bring to a boil over medium-high heat. Add carrots; cook just until tender-crisp to bite (about 30 seconds). Drain.

Cucumber. Cut ½ **English cucumber** into 3 to 4-inch-long julienne strips.

Spinach. Discard stems from 1 pound **spinach**; rinse leaves. Into a 2 to 3-quart pan, pour water to a depth of 1 inch. Bring to a boil over high heat. Add spinach; cook just until limp (about 1 minute). Drain.

Mushrooms. Soak 2 ounces **Oriental dried mushrooms** in warm water to cover just until pliable; drain and rinse. Cut off and discard stems; cut caps into long, thin strips. Place in a small pan along with 2 tablespoons *each* **sugar, soy sauce,** and **water**. Cover and cook over medium heat, stirring occasionally, until liquid is absorbed (about 5 minutes).

Wasabi paste. In a small bowl, stir together 3 tablespoons **wasabi powder** and 3½ teaspoons **water** until smooth. Divide into small portions; let diners mix wasabi with soy to make a dipping sauce.

Hand-shaped Sushi

(Pictured on page 42 and on front cover)

Use half a batch of rice for two types of *nigiri:* stuffed shrimp and flat cakes with bright salmon caviar.

   ½ recipe Sushi Rice (page 43)
       Water
   ¾ **cup seasoned rice vinegar for sushi (or ¾ cup white (distilled) or white wine vinegar mixed with 4½ tablespoons sugar and seasoned to taste with salt)**
  12 **large shrimp**
       Wasabi paste (optional; page 43)
       Pickled red ginger (*shoga*)
       Soy sauce (optional)
   3 **or 4 sheets nori, toasted as directed on page 43**
   1 **or 2 jars (4 oz.** *each*) **salmon caviar**

Prepare ½ recipe Sushi Rice, using 1½ cups rice and 1¾ cups water (cooking time remains the same). Season rice as directed, using ¼ cup of the seasoned vinegar. Let cool.

Shrimp with Sushi. Devein shrimp by inserting a skewer into back through shell in several places to pull out sand vein. Run a bamboo skewer lengthwise through each unshelled shrimp to keep it from curling as it cooks.

Pour 4 cups water into a deep pan; bring to a boil over high heat. Add shrimp and cook until pink (4 to 6 minutes); drain immediately and let cool. Remove skewers and shell shrimp, leaving tails attached; then butterfly each one by slitting underside almost to (but not through) back. Place in a bowl and add remaining ½ cup seasoned vinegar. Let stand for 30 minutes, then drain.

If desired, dab a bit of wasabi paste inside each shrimp. With moistened fingers, press 1 tablespoon of the rice mixture into each split shrimp. Place on a platter; garnish with ginger. If desired, serve with soy and wasabi paste. Makes 12 sushi-stuffed shrimp.

Sushi Cakes with Salmon Caviar. Cut toasted nori into 1 by 7-inch strips; set aside. Shape remaining rice mixture (about 4½ cups) into 24 golf-ball-size portions, using about 3 tablespoons for each. With the palm of your hand, flatten each portion into a round cake about 2 inches in diameter. While rice is still moist, wrap 1 strip of nori around each cake; strip should be level with bottom and should extend about ¼ inch above top. Spoon 1 to 2 teaspoons caviar atop each cake. Place on platter with shrimp. Makes 24 sushi cakes.

Hand-rolled Sushi

Following directions for **Rolled Sushi** (page 43), prepare **Sushi Rice;** also toast about 14 sheets roasted or unroasted **nori.** With scissors, cut nori into 4 to 5-inch squares. Stack nori on a plate or in a basket. Prepare **Sesame Sauce** (recipe follows). Prepare **wasabi paste** and **vegetables** as directed for Rolled Sushi; also use **fish** as described for Rolled Sushi, but cut into thin slices instead of strips. (If desired, use butterflied cooked shrimp and salmon caviar as described for Hand-shaped Sushi.) Place all ingredients on large tray. To assemble, place a piece of nori in the palm of your hand. Spoon a small quantity of rice into center; top with fish, vegetables, and wasabi paste or Sesame Sauce (don't pile on ingredients too generously). Overlap corners of nori to enclose filling. Dip into **soy sauce** (flavored with wasabi paste, if desired), and eat out of hand. Makes 6 servings.

Sesame Sauce. In a small pan over medium heat, toast 4 teaspoons **sesame seeds,** shaking pan frequently, until golden (about 2 minutes). Place in a bowl and add 1 cup **mayonnaise,** 4 teaspoons **honey,** and 1½ teaspoons **sesame oil.** Stir mixture thoroughly, then spoon into 1 or 2 small serving bowls. Makes about 1 cup.

Steamed Short-grain Rice

At the heart of every Japanese meal is a bowl of steaming short-grain rice. The grains cling together when cooked, making the rice easy to manage with chopsticks. For variety, the Japanese sometimes cook their rice in seasoned broth rather than in water, or add small pieces of fresh vegetables.

   1 **cup short-grain (pearl) rice**
       Cold water
   ½ **teaspoon salt (optional)**

Place rice in a heavy 1½ to 2-quart pan. Cover with water, stir, and drain; repeat until water is clear. To drained rice, add 1¼ cups water and, if desired, salt. Bring to a boil over high heat. Cover, reduce heat to low, and simmer for 20 minutes without lifting cover. Remove from heat and let stand, covered, for 5 to 10 minutes. Uncover and fluff with a fork before serving. Makes about 3½ cups (2 to 4 servings).

Rice with Seasoned Broth

Prepare **Steamed Short-grain Rice,** but omit the 1¼ cups water. Instead, use ½ teaspoon *each* **soy sauce** and grated **fresh ginger,** 2 tablespoons **sake** or dry sherry (optional), and enough **regular-strength chicken broth** or dashi (page 41) to make 1¼ cups liquid.

Rice with Vegetables

Prepare **Steamed Short-grain Rice,** but when mixture comes to a boil, add ½ to ¾ cup **vegetables.** Use fresh or frozen peas, diced carrots, diced celery, or a combination.

Five-flavor Summer Noodles

In Japan, where each season has its specialties, ice-cold noodle soup is a popular dish for the hot summer months. Thin *somen* noodles (kept chilly in ice and water) and shreds of meat and vegetables are added to a slightly sweet broth at the table.

> Water
> 1 whole chicken breast (about 1 lb.)
> Egg Pancakes (recipe follows)
> 3 large Oriental dried mushrooms
> 1 teaspoon sugar
> 2 teaspoons soy sauce
> 1 package (3 oz.) sliced cooked ham
> ½ large cucumber
> Soup Broth (recipe follows)
> Ice cubes
> 2 teaspoons salt
> About 8 ounces somen noodles
> About 1 tablespoon wasabi powder or prepared horseradish (optional)

Into a 2-quart pan, pour water to a depth of 1 inch. Bring to a simmer over medium-low heat. Add chicken and cook, covered, until meat in thickest portion is no longer pink when slashed (about 15 minutes). Let cool. Remove and discard skin and bones. Cut meat diagonally into thin slices; then cut slices into thin shreds about 2 inches long.

Prepare Egg Pancakes; cut into shreds and set aside. Soak mushrooms in warm water to cover just until pliable. Drain and rinse well; cut off and discard stems. In a small pan, combine mushroom caps, ⅓ cup water, sugar, and soy. Cook over medium heat, uncovered, stirring often, until most of the liquid has evaporated. Let cool; then cut into thin shreds.

Cut ham into 2-inch-wide strips, then cut crosswise into thin shreds. Peel cucumber, if desired. Cut diagonally into thin slices; stack slices and cut into thin shreds. Arrange chicken, pancake shreds, mushrooms, ham, and cucumber in separate mounds on a serving plate. (At this point, you may cover and refrigerate for up to 4 hours.)

Shortly before serving, prepare Soup Broth; pour into a pitcher or teapot and set aside. Also half-fill a large serving bowl with ice cubes and a little water.

Into a large kettle, pour 8 cups water; add salt. Bring to a boil over medium-high heat. Add noodles and cook until water returns to a boil. Immediately add 1 cup cold water; cook, uncovered, until water returns to a full boil. Drain noodles; then plunge into a kettle of cold water, stir, and drain again. Repeat 3 or 4 times, but do not drain the last time. Instead, grasp noodles, a bundle at a time, and dip in and out of water until strands are parallel. Arrange noodles in a wavy pattern in serving bowl. If desired, mix wasabi powder with enough water to make a stiff paste; shape into a cone. (Or offer prepared horseradish in a small container.)

To serve, use chopsticks to place a bundle of noodles in each of 4 to 6 individual bowls. Let diners add meat, pancake, and vegetable shreds to bowls; pour broth over all. Add a dab of wasabi paste, if desired; mix thoroughly. Makes 4 to 6 servings.

Egg Pancakes. In a bowl, beat 3 **eggs** with 1 teaspoon **salt** until well blended. Heat an 8 to 9-inch heavy frying pan (preferably one with a nonstick finish) over medium-low heat. When pan is hot, brush with about 1 teaspoon **salad oil.** Using a ¼-cup measure, dip out about 3 tablespoons of the egg. Pour into pan all at once and quickly tilt pan to coat bottom evenly. Cover and cook until set but not browned (about 1 minute). Flip over and cook for about 15 more seconds; then turn out onto a paper towel and let cool. Repeat with remaining egg, brushing pan with oil each time (you can make 2 or 3 more pancakes). Trim edges of pancakes to make them square; discard trimmings and cut pancakes into 2-inch-wide strips. Stack strips and cut crosswise into thin shreds.

Soup Broth. In a bowl, place 3½ cups **dashi** (page 41) or 2 cans (14½ oz. *each*) regular-strength chicken broth (skimmed of fat). Stir in 3 tablespoons **soy sauce;** then stir in ¼ cup **mirin** or 2 teaspoons sugar.

Fish & Shellfish

Seafood & Vegetable Tempura

(Pictured on facing page)

There are two secrets to tempura's light, crunchy coating. The first is the batter—thin, cold, and lumpy (the lumps help give the coating its lacy appearance).The second trick is to serve tempura immediately after cooking; the fragile coating softens upon standing.

> Seafood (suggestions follow)
> Vegetables (suggestions follow)
> Tempura Dipping Sauce (recipe follows)
> About 6 cups salad oil
> Tempura Batter (recipe follows)

Prepare seafood and vegetables and arrange on platters. Prepare Tempura Dipping Sauce and pour it into 4 small individual bowls. Into a wok or deep, heavy pan, pour oil to a depth of 1½ to 2 inches and heat to 375° on a deep-frying thermometer. While oil heats, prepare Tempura Batter.

Using chopsticks or tongs, dip prepared seafood and vegetables, a piece at a time, into batter. Let excess batter drip off, then gently lower into hot oil (cook several pieces at a time; do not crowd in pan). Cook, turning occasionally, until crisp and light golden (2 to 3 minutes). Remove and drain briefly on a wire rack. Serve at once, with sauce for dipping. As you fry, frequently skim and discard any bits of batter from oil. Makes 4 servings.

Seafood. You'll need about 1 pound **large shrimp** or 1 pound **fish** (or a combination of the two). Shell shrimp, leaving tails attached. Split each shrimp along back, cutting almost through shrimp to make it lie flat; remove sand vein. Rinse and pat dry.

For fish, use salmon, sole, or lingcod steaks or fillets. Remove and discard bones and skin; cut fish into 1½ by 3-inch strips about ¼ inch thick.

Vegetables. Choose at least 3 from the following: 2 medium-size **carrots,** cut into 2½ to 3-inch lengths, then into ¼-inch-thick lengthwise slices; ⅓-pound wedge of a large **eggplant,** cut crosswise into ¼-inch-thick slices; 12 large **mushrooms,** cut in half through stems; 1 medium-size **sweet potato,** peeled and cut into ¼-inch-thick rounds; ¼ pound **green beans,** ends removed (cut in half if long).

Tempura Dipping Sauce. In a small pan, combine 1 cup **dashi** (page 41) or 1 bottle (8 oz.) clam juice with ¼ cup *each* **soy sauce** and **dry sherry.** Bring to a boil over medium-high heat; then remove from heat and let cool to room temperature. In separate small bowls, place 3 tablespoons *each* finely shredded **fresh ginger** and **daikon.** Let diners add ginger and daikon to individual bowls of sauce according to taste.

Tempura Batter. In a small bowl, lightly beat together 1 cup plus 2 tablespoons **ice-cold water,** 1 **egg,** and ¼ teaspoon *each* **baking soda** and **salt.** Add 1 cup unsifted **cake flour;** mix just until blended (batter will be lumpy). Sprinkle another ⅓ cup unsifted cake flour over top of batter. With a fork, stir batter 1 or 2 strokes (do not blend thoroughly; most of the last addition of flour should be floating on top). Half-fill a larger bowl with **ice;** set bowl of batter in it to keep batter cold while you cook.

Iced Shrimp & Noodles

Created with the hot days of summer in mind, this cooling concoction is simply shrimp, cucumbers, and icy-cold noodles.

> ½ large cucumber, peeled if desired
> ½ pound small cooked shrimp
> Dipping Sauce (recipe follows)
> Ice cubes
> About 6 ounces somen noodles

Cut cucumber in half lengthwise, then thinly slice crosswise. Arrange with shrimp on a platter.

Prepare Dipping Sauce; pour into 4 small containers. Half-fill 4 individual bowls with ice cubes and a little water.

Prepare noodles as directed for Five-flavor Summer Noodles (page 45); serve into bowls. Pass cucumber and shrimp to add to each serving. To eat, dip foods in sauce. Makes 4 servings.

Dipping Sauce. In a bowl, place 1 cup **dashi** (page 41) or regular-strength chicken broth (skimmed of fat). Add 5 tablespoons **soy sauce;** then stir in ¼ cup **mirin** or cream sherry, or 2 teaspoons sugar.

Seafood & Vegetable Tempura *(Recipe on facing page)* with Shredded Daikon

1 Split shelled shrimp along vein, cutting almost all the way through to make it lie flat.

2 Stir batter only once or twice after adding second portion of flour; most of flour will remain floating on top. Lumpy batter makes light, crisp tempura.

3 Dip shrimp into batter, then let excess drip off. Gently lower into hot oil.

4 Cooked shrimp have crisp, light golden coating. Serve cooked tempura immediately.

The Cooking of Japan 47

Choosing the Freshest Fish

Fish and shellfish have long been staples in the Japanese diet. This reliance on foods from the sea is easy to understand—since Japan is surrounded by ocean (no town is farther than 100 miles from the coast), seafood is in ready supply. Buddhist dietary laws helped to reinforce the importance of fish as a food source; from the mid-16th to late 19th century, the eating of four-footed animals was prohibited.

The Japanese have turned this dietary limitation to distinct advantage, preparing fresh seafood in any number of different and delicious ways. Fish is served steamed, simmered, grilled—and raw, as in sushi (pages 43–44) and sashimi (page 49). But whatever the method, preparation is simple. Cooking (if any) is brief; there are no complex sauces to mask inferior flavor or texture. Because these dishes are so simple, they share an absolute requirement for the very freshest fish. In Japan, just-caught freshness is taken for granted—but in the United States, you'll have to track down a reliable fish market and learn to judge its wares. Once you know the signs, it's easy to distinguish a truly fresh fish from one that's been out of the ocean a bit too long.

Trust your senses. The first indication of good, fresh fish is a mild, pleasant aroma. Don't buy fish with a disagreeable odor—it won't taste any better than it smells. Fresh fish feels firm; the flesh should spring back when gently pressed. If the flesh is slack or has begun to separate from the bone, the fish is no longer fresh.

You can evaluate the overall quality of a market's offerings by examining its whole fish. These should have clear, full (or slightly protruding) eyes; cloudy or sunken eyes indicate that the fish is past its prime. Gills should be pinkish red and free of slime; as the fish ages, the gills turn gray, then brownish or greenish. Skin should be shiny, with unfaded color and pronounced markings. When you're buying steaks or fillets, choose moist pieces that look freshly cut; avoid those that are dry or brown at the edges.

Storing fresh fish. Fresh fish is best used on the day it's bought. If you must store it, wrap it in a leakproof wrapper and refrigerate for no longer than 2 days. (For sushi and sashimi, it's essential to use fish on the day it's purchased—or better still, on the day it's caught.)

Simmered Shellfish

A popular dish for cold, blustery winter days is *yosenabe* ("a bit of everything")—shellfish and vegetables cooked gently in steaming broth.

- **4 ounces bean threads**
- **8 to 10 small live hard-shell clams**
  Salted water
- **8 to 10 large shrimp**
- **1 large cooked Dungeness crab, cleaned**
- **½ small head napa cabbage**
- **½ pound tofu (bean curd)**
- **2 large cans (49½ oz. *each*) regular-strength chicken broth**
- **2 tablespoons Dijon mustard**
- **¼ cup soy sauce**
- **½ cup dry sherry**
- **4 teaspoons grated or minced fresh ginger**
- **1 bunch watercress**

Soak bean threads in warm water to cover for 20 minutes. Meanwhile, scrub clams well with a brush, then soak in salted water for 15 minutes. Drain. Shell and devein shrimp. Lift off and discard back shell from crab. Break off legs and crack; cut body into 4 sections. Cut off and discard stem end from cabbage. Drain tofu, then cut into 1-inch cubes.

Combine broth, mustard, soy, sherry, and ginger in a 5 to 6-quart kettle. Bring to a boil over high heat; cover, reduce heat, and keep broth at a simmer.

Warm a 4-quart covered casserole by rinsing it thoroughly with hottest tap water. Drain bean threads, cut into 5 to 6-inch lengths, and place in casserole; cover and keep warm on an electric warming tray (or wrap in a towel).

Add clams to broth; cover and simmer for 5 minutes. Add shrimp and crab; cook until clams open (about 3 more minutes). Lift seafood from broth and arrange in casserole. Re-cover; keep warm.

Add cabbage to broth and cook just until wilted (about 3 minutes); lift out with tongs and arrange in casserole. Re-cover casserole and keep warm. Reduce heat under kettle so broth steams but no bubbles break the surface. Carefully add tofu and cook for 5 minutes; transfer to casserole. Garnish with watercress. Pour steaming broth into casserole up to level of vegetables and seafood; pour remaining broth into a pitcher to add to casserole as needed. Cover casserole. Place a selection of seafood, vegetables, tofu, and noodles in each of 4 to 6 wide soup plates; ladle in broth. Eat foods with forks or chopsticks; sip broth. Makes 4 to 6 servings.

Grilled Fish

The flavor of white-fleshed fish is enhanced by a delicate teriyaki-like sauce. After marinating, fish cooks quickly in the broiler or on the grill.

- 1 to 1½ pounds firm, white-fleshed fish fillets or steaks (sea bass, halibut, tilefish, or lingcod), *each* ¾ to 1 inch thick
- 3 tablespoons soy sauce
- 2 tablespoons mirin or cream sherry
- 1 tablespoon lemon juice
- 1½ teaspoons salad oil

Wipe fish and pat dry; cut fillets into serving-size pieces (or cut steaks in half lengthwise, discarding bone). For easier handling, run 2 bamboo skewers lengthwise through each piece, about 1 inch apart. In a small bowl, combine soy, mirin, lemon juice, and oil. Brush part of sauce on all sides of fish; reserve remaining sauce.

Place fish on a broiler pan in a preheated broiler 3 to 4 inches below heat (or place on a small, lightly greased grill about 4 inches above a solid bed of glowing coals). Cook, turning once and basting often with remaining sauce, just until flesh inside fish looks opaque (7 to 10 minutes—to test, prod in thickest portion with a fork). Makes 3 or 4 servings.

Salmon Teriyaki

Homemade teriyaki sauce is both marinade and basting sauce for skewered salmon. Serve with Eggplant with Sesame Sauce (page 56).

- About 2 pounds salmon steaks, *each* about 1¼ inches thick
- 1 medium-size onion
- ½ cup soy sauce
- ¼ cup sake or dry sherry
- 1 teaspoon sugar

Cut salmon into 1¼-inch cubes, discarding any bones. Cut onion into quarters; separate into single layers and cut each piece into 1¼-inch squares. Thread salmon cubes and onion squares alternately on bamboo skewers, placing about 4 pieces *each* of salmon and onion on each skewer.

In a small bowl, combine soy, sake, and sugar; stir until sugar is dissolved. Brush skewered salmon and onion generously with some of the soy mixture;

then cover and refrigerate for about 30 minutes.

Place skewers on a lightly greased grill 4 to 6 inches above a solid bed of glowing coals. Cook, turning often and brushing with remaining soy mixture, just until salmon looks opaque in center (about 10 minutes—to test, prod with a fork). Makes 4 to 6 servings.

Sashimi

Classic *sashimi* is a striking presentation: extra-thin slices of rosy raw tuna, pale sea bass, halibut, or albacore arranged atop shredded carrot and snowy daikon, and accompanied by piquant wasabi paste.

- Wasabi paste (page 43)
- 1 large daikon (about 1 lb.), peeled
- ⅓ small carrot
- Ice water
- 1 pound boneless, skinless fresh yellowfin or bluefin tuna, Pacific albacore, white sea bass, or halibut
- Soy sauce

Prepare wasabi paste; place in a small bowl.

Shred daikon into long, fine strands. (If your grater doesn't make long strands, use a vegetable peeler to slice daikon lengthwise into paper-thin strips; then cut strips into slivers with a very sharp knife.) You should have about 3 cups. Shred carrot the same way; mix with daikon. Place vegetables in a bowl; pour in ice water to cover.

Wipe fish lightly with a damp cloth; pat dry with paper towels. Cut away and discard any dark portions of flesh (dark flesh tastes quite strong when raw). If fish is wide, cut lengthwise, with the grain, into 2 or 3 strips (each 1 to 2 inches wide). Place strips on a cutting board. Using a very sharp, thin-bladed knife, cut strips across the grain into ⅛ to ¼-inch slices (as thin as possible). To keep flavor fresh, handle fish no more than necessary.

Drain daikon mixture well. Arrange evenly on a chilled platter. Using a spatula, transfer fish slices to platter, arranging over daikon mixture in rows; leave about a third of the daikon exposed at one end of platter. (The Japanese arrange fish in rows with uneven numbers of slices, such as 9 or 11.)

Place wasabi paste on platter beside fish. Provide diners with individual dishes of soy; let them season soy to taste with wasabi paste, then use the mixture as dipping sauce for fish and vegetables. Makes 6 appetizer or 4 main-dish servings.

 # Poultry

Chicken & Shrimp Noodle Salad

Quick-cooking *chuka soba* noodles are tossed with sesame oil, then topped with vegetables and meat.

> 2 **tablespoons sesame seeds**
> **Salad Dressing (recipe follows)**
> About ⅓ **pound medium-size shrimp, shelled and deveined**
> 1 **whole chicken breast (about 1 lb.)**
> ½ **large cucumber**
> 2½ **cups bean sprouts**
> 2 **teaspoons salt**
> 4 **ounces chuka soba noodles**
> 1 **tablespoon sesame oil**
> ½ **cup sliced green onions (including tops)**

In a small frying pan over medium heat, toast sesame seeds, shaking pan frequently, until golden (about 2 minutes). Prepare Salad Dressing; set aside.

Pour 2 cups water into a small pan; bring to a boil over high heat. Add shrimp; reduce heat and simmer until pink (4 to 6 minutes). Drain; let cool. Cook chicken as directed for Five-flavor Summer Noodles (page 45). Cut into bite-size pieces. Peel cucumber. Cut in half lengthwise; slice crosswise.

Half-fill a 5-quart kettle with water; bring to a boil over high heat. Place bean sprouts in a wire strainer and dip into boiling water for about 30 seconds. Remove and rinse with cold water. Add salt to boiling water in kettle; drop in noodles and cook, uncovered, until water returns to a full boil and noodles float to top (1 to 2 minutes). Drain noodles at once; rinse with cold water until only slightly warm. Drain again. Pour onto a rimmed serving plate and drizzle with oil; toss until coated.

Arrange shrimp, chicken, cucumber, and bean sprouts on top of noodles. Drizzle dressing over salad and toss until well blended; sprinkle with onions and sesame seeds. Makes about 6 servings.

Salad Dressing. In a small bowl, combine 2 tablespoons **soy sauce**, ⅓ cup **rice vinegar**, 2 tablespoons **sugar**, ¼ teaspoon **dry mustard**, and, if desired, a dash of **ground red pepper** (cayenne). Stir to blend.

Turkey & Vegetable Pot Dish

Here's one tasty member of the family of Japanese dishes called *nabemono* ("things in a pot"). Simmering broth, gingery ground turkey balls, and fresh vegetables add up to a satisfying one-dish meal.

> About 2 **ounces bean threads**
> **Ground Turkey Balls (recipe follows)**
> 4 **cups regular-strength chicken broth mixed with 2 cups water, or 6 cups dashi (page 41)**
> 2 **teaspoons soy sauce**
> 2 **medium-size carrots, cut diagonally into ⅛-inch-thick slices**
> 6 **large napa cabbage leaves, cut into 2-inch squares**
> 6 **to 8 green onions (including tops), cut into 2-inch lengths**
> 8 **fresh shiitake mushrooms or button mushrooms (cut in half if large)**

Soak bean threads in warm water to cover for 30 minutes; drain, cut into 4 to 5-inch lengths, and set aside. Prepare Ground Turkey Balls; set aside.

Pour broth-water mixture and soy into a 4 to 5-quart kettle; bring to a boil over high heat. Add turkey balls. When broth returns to a boil, reduce heat to medium and simmer for 4 minutes, skimming foam from top. Then, without stirring, add in sequence: carrots, cabbage, onions, mushrooms, and bean threads. (Allow broth to return to a simmer between additions.) Cover and simmer until carrots are tender to bite (about 1 minute); remove from heat. Divide ingredients among 4 soup bowls and pour broth over all. Makes 4 servings.

Ground Turkey Balls. In a bowl, combine 1 pound **ground turkey**, 1 teaspoon grated **fresh ginger**, 1 tablespoon **cornstarch**, 1 tablespoon **sake** or dry sherry, and 1 teaspoon **salt**. Add 1 **egg**, lightly beaten, and stir well. Shape into 1½-inch balls.

Chicken & Egg on Rice

Like the French omelet, Japanese *donburi* is a nutritious, spur-of-the-moment supper that's ideal for one or two diners. It's always served over a bowl of rice. In fact, the Japanese use a special donburi bowl—it's larger than a regular rice bowl, and fitted with a lid.

4 or 5 Oriental dried mushrooms
Steamed Short-grain Rice (page 44)
2 tablespoons salad oil
¼ cup sliced green onions (including tops)
6 to 8 ounces boneless chicken (1 whole skinned, boned breast or 2 skinned, boned thighs), cut into bite-size pieces
¼ cup regular-strength chicken broth
2 tablespoons sake or dry sherry
2 tablespoons mirin or cream sherry
2 tablespoons soy sauce
1 teaspoon grated or minced fresh ginger
2 eggs

Soak mushrooms in warm water to cover for 30 minutes; drain. Cut off and discard stems, then cut caps into slices.

Prepare Steamed Short-grain Rice; keep warm. Heat 1 tablespoon of the oil in a small (about 4-inch) pan over medium-high heat. Add half the mushrooms and 2 tablespoons of the onions and cook, stirring, until lightly browned (about 1 minute). Add half the chicken and cook, stirring, until lightly browned (1 to 2 more minutes). Add 2 tablespoons of the broth, 1 tablespoon *each* of the sake, mirin, and soy, and ½ teaspoon of the ginger. Cook, stirring, until about ⅛ inch of sauce remains in pan.

In a small bowl, lightly beat 1 of the eggs. Reduce heat to low and gradually pour egg into bubbling sauce, stirring to distribute it through sauce. Cover and cook just until egg is set (about 1 minute). Divide rice between two small serving bowls. Run a small spatula around edge of egg mixture and slide onto one bowl of rice. Repeat cooking with remaining oil, mushrooms, onions, chicken, broth, sake, mirin, soy, ginger, and egg. Slide onto second bowl of rice. Makes 2 servings.

Skewered Chicken

Yaki (grilled) plus *tori* (chicken) yields *yakitori*: chicken breast strips threaded on skewers, then briefly grilled. Serve as an entrée or as an appetizer.

3 whole chicken breasts (about 3 lbs. *total*), split, skinned, and boned
About 12 green onions (white part only)
⅓ cup dry sherry
2 tablespoons soy sauce
½ teaspoon minced fresh ginger
1 clove garlic, minced or pressed

Cut each breast half crosswise into 4 equal strips, each about 1 inch wide. Cut onions into 1½-inch lengths. Thread 4 pieces *each* of chicken and onion alternately on each skewer. (Fold long pieces of chicken in two before threading on skewers.) In a bowl, combine sherry, soy, ginger, and garlic.

Place skewers on a lightly greased grill about 4 inches above a solid bed of medium-glowing coals (or place on a broiler pan about 4 inches below heat). Cook, turning once and basting often with sherry mixture, until meat is no longer pink when slashed (6 to 8 minutes). Makes 3 or 4 servings.

Seasoned Fried Chicken

With characteristic regard for presentation, the Japanese have devised a delicate-looking and tasting version of the familiar fried chicken.

1½ cups coarse bread crumbs (*pan ko*), purchased or homemade (page 55)
3 whole chicken breasts (about 3 lbs. *total*), skinned and boned
½ cup soy sauce
1 tablespoon *each* grated or minced fresh ginger and lemon juice
2 tablespoons sake or dry sherry
6 tablespoons all-purpose flour
2 tablespoons cornstarch
2 eggs
Salad oil

Prepare bread crumbs and place in a pie pan.

Cut chicken into 1-inch-square chunks. In a bowl, combine soy, ginger, lemon juice, and sake; stir in chicken. Cover and let stand at room temperature for about 30 minutes, stirring occasionally. Drain chicken and pat dry; pour marinade through a wire strainer and reserve. In a pie pan, combine flour and cornstarch. In another pie pan, lightly beat eggs. Dredge chicken pieces in flour mixture; shake off excess. Dip in egg and roll in crumbs.

Meanwhile, pour oil into a 2½ to 3-quart pan to a depth of 2 inches and heat to 375° on a deep-frying thermometer. Fry chicken, a few pieces at a time, until coating is browned on all sides and meat is no longer pink in center when slashed (about 2 minutes). Drain briefly on paper towels and serve immediately, offering reserved marinade in a small bowl for dipping. Makes 4 to 6 servings.

Tabletop Cooking for Family and Guests

The Japanese enjoy a variety of tabletop meals. *Sukiyaki*—quick-cooked meat and vegetables—is one popular choice. Beef is preferred for this dish, but since it's costly in Japan, pork or chicken is often used instead. Whichever meat you choose, rush sukiyaki from pan to plate.

In the chilly winter, the table often holds a pot of steaming broth and platters of raw food; diners cook and assemble their meals on the spot. Try our *udon-suki* and enjoy this warming festive approach to dining. Other candidates for this style of cooking include Simmered Shellfish (page 48), Turkey & Vegetable Pot Dish (page 50), and Simmered Beef with Vegetables (page 54).

Teppan (griddle) cooking is popular in restaurants in Japan; we offer an unusual teppan-style savory pancake called *okonomiyaki*.

Any of these dishes is a meal in itself. Tea, sake, and beer are good beverage choices; offer fresh fruit or fruit sherbet for dessert.

Sukiyaki

    Cooking Sauce (recipe follows)
2 **pounds lean boneless beef (sirloin) or pork shoulder steak (1¼ to 1½ inches thick); or 3 pounds chicken breasts, boned and skinned; or a combination of 2 or 3 meats**
    About 1 pound medium-firm tofu (bean curd)
1 **can (about 1 lb.) boiled yam noodles or alimentary paste (*shirataki*) or 4 ounces bean threads**
1 **can (about 6 oz.) whole or cut bamboo shoots, thinly sliced**
½ **pound mushrooms, sliced**
8 **to 10 green onions (including tops), cut into 2-inch lengths**
1 **bunch watercress or spinach (tough stems removed)**
4 **to 6 eggs (optional)**

Prepare Cooking Sauce; set aside.

Trim fat from beef or pork; reserve two 1 by 2-inch strips of fat and discard remainder. Remove and discard any bones. Wrap meat and place in freezer for about 30 minutes; then cut diagonally across the grain into ⅛-inch-thick slices. Place on a platter; arrange reserved strips of fat on top. (Or cut chicken into long, thin strips; place on a platter.)

Drain tofu in a colander for at least 15 minutes, then wrap in a towel and place a flat, heavy weight on top. Let stand for about 30 minutes. Cut into 1-inch squares.

Rinse and drain yam noodles. If using bean threads, soak in warm water to cover for 30 minutes; drain. Cut into 5 to 6-inch lengths.

Arrange tofu, noodles, bamboo shoots, mushrooms, onions, and watercress on platters.

To cook at the table, you'll need a wide electric frying pan or a wide sukiyaki pan or frying pan set over a portable tabletop cook unit. Arrange meat, vegetables, and Cooking Sauce near cooking pan.

Heat pan over medium-high heat and add strips of fat (if using chicken only, use 1 to 2 tablespoons salad oil). Stir strips around pan until pan is coated with fat; remove and discard. Add about half the meat and cook, turning frequently, until lightly browned; push to one corner of pan. Pour about a fourth of the Cooking Sauce over meat. Add about half the tofu, noodles, mushrooms, bamboo shoots, onions, and watercress, keeping each ingredient in a separate pile. Pour another fourth of the cooking sauce over all. Simmer, turning frequently, until vegetables are soft and tofu and noodles have absorbed some of the sauce (about 5 minutes).

Reduce heat to low and spoon sukiyaki onto individual plates, emptying pan. To serve seconds, raise heat to medium-high and add remaining meat, pouring about half the remaining sauce over it. Add remaining ingredients and sauce and cook as directed above.

If desired, lightly beat 1 egg in each of 4 to 6 small bowls; let diners use as a dip for meat and vegetables. Makes 4 to 6 servings.

Cooking Sauce. In a small bowl, stir together 1⅔ cups **water**, ¾ cup **soy sauce**, ⅓ cup **mirin** or cream sherry, and 3 tablespoons **sugar**. Pour into a small pitcher.

Udon-suki

    Pork Balls (recipe follows)
    Prepared vegetables (suggestions follow)
    About 1 dozen small live hard-shell clams
3 **packages (about 7 oz. *each*) fresh udon noodles (or about 6 ounces dry udon or spaghetti)**
    Boiling salted water
1 **tablespoon salad oil**
2 **large cans (49½ oz. *each*) regular-strength chicken broth**

Prepare Pork Balls and vegetables. Scrub clams well with a brush and rinse with cold water.

Shortly before serving, drop fresh noodles into a large quantity of boiling salted water. Cook until tender (2 to 3 minutes); drain. (Or cook dry noodles according to package directions; drain.) Mix noodles with oil. Place in a serving bowl.

Pour about half the broth (plus pan juices from Pork Balls) into an electric wok or frying pan; or use a kettle over a portable tabletop cook unit. Bring to a boil; then seat diners at the table. (If you're using canned heat or

alcohol, pour all broth into a 4 to 5-quart kettle. Bring to a boil over high heat; then pour about half into your table cooker. Keep remaining broth hot in the kitchen.)

At the table, place half the clams in the cooking pan. Cover and cook until broth returns to boil; reduce heat and simmer for about 3 minutes. Then add about half the Pork Balls and half the vegetables (or enough for each diner to have a serving). Cook until clams open. Divide cooked ingredients equally among individual bowls; then ladle some of the hot broth into each bowl. For second servings, replenish cooker with remaining broth and add remaining ingredients. Cook as directed above. Makes 4 to 6 servings.

Pork Balls. In a small frying pan over medium heat, toast ¼ cup **pine nuts,** shaking pan frequently, until golden (about 4 minutes). Place in a bowl and add 1 pound **ground pork,** 1 **egg,** 2 tablespoons **all-purpose flour,** 1 tablespoon **soy sauce,** and ½ teaspoon grated **fresh ginger.** Mix well. Shape into balls, using about 1 tablespoon meat mixture for each; arrange slightly apart on a rimmed baking sheet. Bake in a 475° oven for about 15 minutes or until no longer pink when slashed. Reserve any pan juices to add to broth. Makes about 36 meatballs.

Prepared vegetables. Choose at least 4 from the following; you'll need a total of 6 to 8 cups vegetables.

Carrots or celery. Cut diagonally into ¼-inch-thick slices. Into a wide frying pan, pour water to a depth of ½ inch; bring to a boil over high heat. Add vegetable and cook just until tender to bite (about 5 minutes); drain and place on a platter.

Daikon or turnips. Peel and cut crosswise into ¼-inch-thick slices. Into a wide frying pan, pour water to a depth of ½ inch; bring to a boil over high heat. Add vegetable and cook just until tender to bite (about 3 minutes for daikon, about 4 minutes for turnips). Drain and arrange on a platter.

Edible-pod peas. Remove and discard ends and strings. Pour 12 cups water into a 5-quart kettle; bring to a boil over high heat. Add peas and cook just until tender-crisp to bite (about 30 seconds). Drain and arrange on a platter.

Leeks or green onions. Trim and discard root ends and tops from leeks, leaving about 1½ inches of green leaves. Discard tough outer leaves. Split leeks lengthwise. Hold each half under cold running water, separating layers to rinse out dirt. Cut root ends from onions and trim tops to about 4 inches. Into a wide frying pan, pour water to a depth of ½ inch; bring to a boil over high heat. Add leeks or onions and cook just until tender when pierced (5 to 8 minutes for leeks, about 1 minute for onions). Drain and arrange on a platter.

Oriental dried mushrooms or fresh button mushrooms. Soak dried mushrooms in warm water to cover for 30 minutes; drain. Cut off and discard stems; leave caps whole. Cut fresh mushrooms lengthwise into ¼-inch-thick slices.

Shrimp & Vegetable Pancakes

⅔ cup dried shrimp or small cooked shrimp
  Teriyaki Sauce (recipe follows)
1⅓ cups water
4 eggs
2 cups all-purpose flour
1⅓ cups *each* chopped green onions (including tops) and finely chopped green cabbage
⅔ cup chopped skinned, boned raw chicken breast
¼ cup slivered pickled red ginger (*shoga*)
  Salad oil
6 to 12 raw egg yolks (optional)
  Dried bonito flakes (*katsuobushi;* optional)
  Prepared seaweed (*aonori;* optional)

Soak dried shrimp in cold water to cover for 20 minutes; drain. Prepare Teriyaki Sauce and set aside.

In a large bowl, beat water and eggs with a fork. Add flour and stir until smooth. Mix in ⅓ cup of the onions; then add cabbage, shrimp, chicken, and ginger.

Cook pancakes at the table, using an electric griddle, an electric frying pan, or a wide frying pan on a portable tabletop cook unit. Turn heat to medium-high; lightly oil cooking surface.

To make small pancakes, use ⅓ cup of the batter for each pancake. Spoon onto griddle and spread to form a 5-inch circle; make as many pancakes at a time as will fit on griddle without touching. Cook until bottoms are golden and tops begin to dry (about 3 minutes); turn with a wide spatula. Generously coat tops of pancakes with Teriyaki Sauce. Sprinkle each pancake with an equal portion of remaining 1 cup onions; if using egg yolks, arrange onions in a circle around edges of each pancake and slip 1 yolk into center. When pancake bottoms are golden, transfer pancakes to individual plates. Pass remaining Teriyaki Sauce. If desired, accompany with bonito flakes and seaweed. Makes 6 servings of 2 pancakes each.

To make large pancakes, use ⅔ cup of the batter for each pancake (cook pancakes 1 at a time). Spoon onto griddle and spread to form an 8-inch circle; cook and serve as directed for small pancakes, allowing 1 whole pancake for each diner. Makes 6 servings of 1 pancake each.

Teriyaki Sauce. In a small pan, mix 3 tablespoons **sugar** and 2 teaspoons **cornstarch** until smooth. Add ½ cup **sake** or dry sherry and ¼ cup **soy sauce.** Place over high heat and stir constantly until mixture boils and thickens. Pour into a serving bowl; use hot or at room temperature.

 # Meats

Simmered Beef with Vegetables

The soft, swishing sound of meat cooking gently in simmering broth gives *shabu-shabu* its name. It's a hearty and rib-sticking combination of beef, vegetables, and noodles cooked briefly in a rich broth.

> 3 cans (14½ oz. *each*) regular-strength beef broth
> ¼ cup soy sauce
> 3 tablespoons sake or dry sherry
> Sesame Sauce (recipe follows)
> 3 or 4 eggs
> About 3 ounces chuka soba, soba, or somen noodles
> 3 or 4 mushrooms
> 3 or 4 green onions (including tops), cut in half lengthwise
> ½ pound spinach, rinsed well
> ½ pound lean boneless beef (sirloin or top round), cut across the grain into ⅛-inch-thick slices

Pour broth, soy, and sake into a 5 to 6-quart kettle. Bring to a boil over high heat; then cover and reduce heat, keeping broth at a simmer.

Prepare Sesame Sauce; set aside. Place eggs in a small pan and add water to cover. Then remove eggs and bring water to a simmer over high heat. Return eggs to pan; reduce heat and simmer, uncovered, for exactly 5 minutes. Plunge immediately into cold water; let stand for 2 minutes. Peel eggs. Place in a bowl; add hottest tap water to cover.

Warm a 2-quart covered casserole by rinsing it with hottest tap water.

Add noodles to simmering broth. Cook, stirring with a fork, for 3 minutes. Lift out and place in casserole; cover and keep warm on an electric warming tray (or wrap in a towel). Add mushrooms to broth; cook for 2 minutes. Transfer to casserole; re-cover and keep warm. Add onions and spinach to broth and cook just until onions are soft (about 1 minute); transfer to casserole. Re-cover and keep warm. Add beef to broth and cook, stirring, until pale in color (about 30 seconds); lift out and arrange in casserole. Pour in steaming broth up to level of

beef. Lift eggs from water and cut about ½ inch off large end of each; set upright in casserole. Cover and present at the table. To serve, place 1 egg and a selection of meat, vegetables, and noodles in each of 3 or 4 wide soup plates; ladle in broth. Serve Sesame Sauce as a dip for meat and vegetables. Eat foods, then sip broth. Makes 3 or 4 servings.

Sesame Sauce. In a wide frying pan over medium heat, toast ½ cup **sesame seeds**, shaking pan frequently, until golden (about 2 minutes). Place in a blender or food processor with ¼ cup of the **cooking broth**, 3 tablespoons **rice vinegar**, 1 teaspoon **sugar**, 1½ tablespoons **soy sauce**, and 1 tablespoon **dry sherry**; whirl until liquefied. Force through a wire strainer, then place in small individual serving bowls.

Beef & Gobo Sticks

Thin strips of marinated beef are wrapped around sticks of gobo—the crunchy root of the burdock plant—to make neat packages called *yahati maki*.

> ¾ pound lean boneless beef (sirloin or top round)
> ¼ cup soy sauce
> ¼ cup mirin or cream sherry
> About ¾ pound gobo (also called burdock)
> 4 cups water
> 1 tablespoon vinegar

Cut beef across the grain into ⅛-inch-thick slices.

To make marinade, heat soy and mirin in a small pan until warm. Remove from heat. Add beef to marinade; let stand for 30 minutes.

Scrub gobo with a brush, then scrape off and discard brown skin. Rinse well. Cut into 5-inch lengths; then cut lengthwise into ⅛-inch-thick strips. Bring water and vinegar to a boil in a 2 to 3-quart pan. Add gobo; cover, reduce heat, and cook until tender to bite (about 5 minutes). Drain.

Hold 4 or 5 gobo strips in a bundle; wrap a beef strip spirally around bundle, covering all gobo. Stretch meat slightly as you go. If necessary, use more than 1 strip, overlapping ends. Squeeze bundle to press meat firmly to gobo; return to marinade. Repeat with remaining gobo and beef.

Remove bundles from marinade and place on a broiler pan in a preheated broiler 2 to 3 inches below heat (or place on a grill about 4 inches above a solid bed of glowing coals). Cook, turning as needed, until lightly browned (3 to 4 minutes). Cut each bundle into 2 or 3 pieces. Makes about 4 servings.

Pork Cutlet

A popular dish in Japan today, *tonkatsu* appeals to Western diners as well. *Pan ko*, the coarse bread crumbs used for coating the pork, are available in Japanese markets; you can also make your own.

    1 to 1½ cups coarse bread crumbs (*pan ko*),
       purchased or homemade (recipe follows)
       Tonkatsu Sauce, purchased or homemade
       (recipe follows)
    1 to 1½ pounds pork chops or steaks, cut ½
       inch thick
    1 egg
    1 tablespoon water
       Salt and pepper
       About 2 tablespoons all-purpose flour
       Salad oil
    2 cups finely shredded cabbage
    ½ cup shredded carrot

Prepare bread crumbs; set aside. Also prepare Tonkatsu Sauce and set aside.

Trim and discard fat and bones from pork. Place meat between sheets of wax paper and pound with a mallet until about ¼ inch thick (overlap any small pieces and pound together into a single piece).

In a shallow bowl, lightly beat egg with water. Spread crumbs on a piece of wax paper. Sprinkle each cutlet lightly with salt and pepper; dust with flour, then shake off excess. Dip cutlets into egg, let drain briefly, and press into crumbs to coat thickly all over. Set aside for 10 minutes to dry slightly.

Into a wide frying pan, pour oil to a depth of ½ inch and heat to 360° on a deep-frying thermometer. Fry cutlets 1 or 2 at a time, turning as needed, until golden brown on both sides (about 5 minutes). Drain briefly on paper towels. Place each cutlet on a dinner plate (if serving with chopsticks, cut each cutlet into 2 or 3 pieces; reassemble on plates). Arrange cabbage and carrot alongside cutlets; offer Tonkatsu Sauce at the table. Makes 3 or 4 servings.

Coarse bread crumbs. Remove crusts from 6 slices **firm-textured white bread.** Cut bread into cubes and whirl in a food processor or blender just until evenly coarse crumbs form. Spread on a rimmed baking sheet and bake in a 325° oven, stirring often, for 15 to 20 minutes or until crisp and dry but not browned. Let cool. If made ahead, store airtight at room temperature for up to 2 months. Makes 2 cups.

Tonkatsu Sauce. Stir together ½ cup **catsup** and 2 tablespoons *each* **Worcestershire** and **soy sauce**.

Sipping Sake

In France and Italy, there are grapes aplenty for making wine; in Holland, Germany, and the British Isles, malt and hops are made into superlative beers. In Japan, rice is the most plentiful commodity, so it's only natural that the brewing of rice wine—*sake* (pronounced sa-KEH)—arose there.

Sake is more than a popular beverage; it's also widely used in cooking. Like dry sherry in Chinese cooking, it contributes a clean, subtle flavor to soups and sauces.

Brewing sake. Sake is produced by a relatively quick and simple operation. First, a starter is introduced into steamed rice. The rice is then allowed to ferment for 3 to 4 weeks; after that, it's pressed, filtered, and bottled. Unlike grape-based wine, sake is not aged; in general, a whole year's bottling is sold before the following year's crop of rice has been harvested.

Several grades of sake are brewed in Japan. Most of what is exported is of very good quality—medium or slightly higher grade. If you visit Japan, though, you can sample some of the special class sake that's produced in quantities too small for export. (Not all sake sold in the United States is imported from Japan; good sake is produced in California, too.)

Serving sake. Sake has a light, clean taste that most people enjoy at first sip. For a touch of Japanese charm and ceremony, serve sake warmed, using traditional serving pieces.

You can warm sake in the bottle; it's traditional, though, to pour it into a *tokkuri* (small stoneware or porcelain pitcher for serving sake) or other heat-resistant vessel. Place the pitcher (or opened sake bottle) in a pan; add water until the level is even with the surface of sake in container. Heat over medium-low heat until water begins to simmer; then remove from heat and let stand until ready to serve (5 to 10 minutes—body temperature or slightly warmer is pleasant for sipping). Wipe pitcher or bottle dry before serving. Many tokkuri come in sets with tiny cups (called *sakazuki*) that hold one or two sips' worth each. Small teacups without handles or small glasses are good substitutes for these.

Many people also like sake at room temperature or over ice. Whatever temperature you choose for serving, toast other diners with a hearty *kampai!* before sipping.

# Vegetables, Eggs & Tofu

Eggplant with Sesame Sauce

Small, elongated "Oriental" eggplant aren't exclusively a vegetable of the Orient—but the Japanese may have devised the best method of cooking them. Quick frying in a shallow layer of oil produces soft and creamy eggplant that absorbs virtually no fat.

> 8 Oriental eggplant, *each* about 6 inches long and 2 inches in diameter (about 2 lbs. *total*)
> Salad oil
> 1 tablespoon sesame seeds
> ¼ cup *each* regular-strength chicken broth and soy sauce
> ½ teaspoon grated fresh ginger

Trim and discard ends from eggplant. In each one, make four ⅓-inch-deep lengthwise slashes, extending to within ½ inch of ends and spaced evenly around eggplant.

Into a wide frying pan or large, heavy pan, pour oil to a depth of ¾ inch and heat to 350° on a deep-frying thermometer. Slip several eggplant into oil; cook, turning occasionally, until soft when pressed (about 4 minutes). Drain; keep warm in a 200° oven. Repeat with remaining eggplant.

In a small frying pan over medium heat, toast sesame seeds, shaking pan frequently, until golden (about 2 minutes). Place in a bowl; stir in broth, soy, and ginger. Pour into a small serving bowl; spoon over cooked eggplant. Makes 4 servings.

Eggplant with Sherry Sauce

Cut and cook eggplant as directed for **Eggplant with Sesame Sauce;** keep warm in a 200° oven.

In a small pan, mix 1 tablespoon **cornstarch** with 2 tablespoons **soy sauce.** Stir until smooth; then gradually stir in 1 cup **regular-strength chicken broth** and ¼ cup **dry sherry.** Cook over medium heat, stirring, until sauce boils and thickens. Spoon sauce over eggplant and sprinkle with 2 tablespoons *each* minced **green onion** (including top) and grated **daikon.** Makes 4 servings.

Quick-fried Gobo

In the United States, gobo is known as burdock, a common weed. In Japan, though, it's a cultivated crop (once believed to have medicinal properties). It has a crunchy texture and a flavor that's compatible with typical Japanese seasonings—as in this classic dish, *kimpira.* (You can buy gobo at Oriental markets.)

> 1 tablespoon sesame seeds
> 4 cups water
> 1 tablespoon vinegar
> About 1 pound gobo (also called burdock)
> 2 tablespoons soy sauce
> 2 tablespoons mirin or cream sherry
> 1 teaspoon sugar
> Few drops of liquid hot pepper seasoning
> 2 tablespoons salad oil
> Sliced green onions (including tops)

In a small frying pan over medium heat, toast sesame seeds, shaking pan frequently, until golden (about 2 minutes). Set aside.

In a bowl, combine water and vinegar. Scrub gobo with a brush, then scrape off and discard brown skin. Rinse well. With a small knife, slice down sides of gobo the way you'd sharpen a pencil, cutting root into shavings. Drop cut pieces immediately into vinegar water.

In a small bowl, combine soy, mirin, sugar, and hot pepper seasoning. Heat oil in a wide frying pan over medium heat. When oil is hot, lift gobo from vinegar water and drain briefly; then add to pan. Cook, stirring, for 1 minute. Add soy mixture and cook, stirring, until gobo is glazed and tender-crisp to bite (5 to 6 minutes). Sprinkle with sesame seeds and onions. Makes 4 to 6 servings.

Iced Sweet Onions

Squeezing and soaking alters the flavor of sliced onions, just as cooking does. Squeezing in cold water draws the heat out and makes them sweet; soaking in ice water makes them crisp. Serve these crunchy onions as a vegetable or a relish.

> 2 medium-size onions, thinly sliced
> Cold water
> Ice cubes

Place onions in a bowl and add cold water to cover. Press and squeeze with your hands until onions are almost limp (3 to 5 minutes). Drain and return to bowl. Add ice cubes and water to cover, using 2 parts water to 1 part ice. Let stand at room temperature until firm (about 30 minutes). Drain well. Makes about 4 servings.

Steamed Savory Custards

In Japan, these delicate custards would be cooked in special ceramic cups—shaped like Western custard cups, but taller and equipped with loose-fitting lids. You can use any heat-resistant 1-cup dishes, though: bowls, regular custard cups, or large coffee cups or mugs.

- 8 edible-pod peas
- 1 medium-size carrot, thinly sliced
- ½ cup thinly sliced mushrooms
- 2 cups regular-strength chicken broth
- 6 eggs
- 2 teaspoons soy sauce
- 1 teaspoon *each* dry sherry (optional) and sugar
- ¼ teaspoon salt
  Sesame oil or salad oil
- ½ to ⅔ cup meat, seafood, or a combination (suggestions follow)
- 2 or 3 spinach leaves, shredded, or 12 small watercress sprigs
- 6 thin slices fresh ginger or 3 paper-thin lemon slices, halved

Into a 2-quart pan, pour water to a depth of 3 inches. Bring to a boil over high heat; add peas and cook just until water returns to a boil (about 30 seconds). Lift out peas; cut crosswise into ¼-inch-wide strips. Add carrot to water in pan; bring to a boil and boil until tender-crisp to bite (2 to 3 minutes). Drain, discarding water. In a small bowl, combine peas, carrot, and mushrooms; set aside.

Pour broth into pan and bring to steaming over high heat. In a large bowl, beat eggs, soy, sherry (if used), sugar, and salt until blended. Slowly pour broth into bowl, beating constantly.

Lightly oil six 8-ounce containers. Distribute vegetable mixture, meat, and spinach evenly among containers; pour in egg mixture and stir gently with a fork. Place a slice of ginger in center of each. Cover

containers loosely with wax paper or foil.

Set a rack in an electric frying pan with a domed lid or in a covered roasting pan. Pour in hot water to a depth of ½ inch. Place containers on rack; bring water to a full boil over high heat, then adjust heat so that water boils gently. Cover and cook just until custards are softly set (8 to 12 minutes—time varies with shape of cooking dishes). To test for doneness, insert a metal spoon about ½ inch into center of custard; if custard is set, it will break and a little clear liquid may flow into the depression. Serve hot. Makes 6 servings.

Meat or seafood. Choose 1 or more from the following: sliced **ham,** cut into slivers; bite-size pieces of **cooked chicken** or turkey; **small cooked shrimp;** fresh or frozen **crabmeat;** bite-size pieces of baked or poached **mild-flavored, white-fleshed fish** or salmon.

Spinach Omelet

This Japanese omelet isn't the familiar filled, folded variety; it's a soft, tender dish of beaten eggs cooked in a slightly sweet mixture of soy sauce, spinach, and onions. Add rice and a fresh-fruit dessert for a quick and thrifty meal.

- 1 bunch (about ¾ lb.) spinach, stems removed
- 3 tablespoons salad oil
- 1 large onion, thinly sliced
- ¼ cup soy sauce
- 1½ tablespoons sugar
- 1¼ cups regular-strength chicken broth
- 6 eggs
  Hot cooked rice

Rinse spinach thoroughly; pat dry with paper towels and set aside.

Heat oil in a 10-inch frying pan over medium-high heat; add onion and cook, stirring, until soft. In a bowl, combine soy, sugar, and broth; pour into pan and bring to a boil. Add spinach; cover and cook until wilted (about 1 minute). Uncover and continue cooking until only ½ inch of sauce remains in pan.

Reduce heat to low and distribute vegetables evenly in pan. In a bowl, beat eggs lightly; then pour over vegetable mixture. Stir gently; cover and cook until eggs are softly set (about 3 minutes).

Spoon egg-vegetable mixture over rice; spoon sauce over all. Makes 4 to 6 servings.

Spinach & Egg Bundles (Recipe on facing page) with Rice Crackers

1 To make egg pancakes, first pour a portion of egg mixture, all at once, into hot oiled pan.

2 With your other hand, immediately tilt pan so egg mixture evenly coats bottom of pan. Cook just until egg is set and feels dry on top.

3 Place shrimp filling in center of wrapper; then gather edges up around filling so bundle resembles a little sack.

4 Wind long-stemmed spinach leaf around top of sack; tie to secure.

Spinach & Egg Bundles

(Pictured on facing page)

These filled bundles make a dramatic opening for a special meal. Cool, gingery shrimp salad awaits diners inside a tender egg wrapper tied with a spinach "ribbon."

Shrimp Salad (recipe follows)
4 or 5 eggs
Water
Salad oil
12 to 16 large spinach leaves with stems, rinsed well

Prepare Shrimp Salad; refrigerate.

In a small bowl, beat eggs; pour into a measuring cup and add 1 to 2 tablespoons water, if necessary, to make 1 cup. Heat a nonstick frying pan measuring 10 inches across the bottom over medium-low heat. Brush 1 teaspoon oil over bottom and slightly up sides. When pan is hot, pour in ¼ cup egg mixture and quickly tilt pan to coat bottom evenly. Cook just until egg is set and feels dry on top; turn out onto a plate lined with paper towels. Repeat with remaining egg mixture, stacking wrappers as you cook them. (Because wrappers tear easily, you may wish to make 1 or 2 extra. For each extra wrapper, add 1 egg and 1½ teaspoons water to egg mixture.)

Pour 8 cups water into a wide frying pan; bring to a boil over high heat. Add 4 spinach leaves, choosing those with the longest stems (total length of leaves should be 10 to 12 inches). Push under water; cook just until leaves are wilted and stems are pliable (about 30 seconds). Rinse with cold water, drain, and set aside.

To assemble, divide Shrimp Salad into 4 portions. Place 1 portion in center of each egg wrapper. Gently gather edges of wrapper at top of filling, so bundle resembles a little sack. Carefully wind a wilted spinach leaf around "neck" of sack and knot to secure—you may need help from an extra pair of hands. (At this point, you may cover and refrigerate until next day.)

Trim stems from remaining spinach leaves. Line each of 4 plates with 2 or 3 leaves; set a bundle on each plate. Makes 4 servings.

Shrimp Salad. Cut 1 small **cucumber** (peeled, if desired) in half lengthwise; scoop out and discard seeds. Thinly slice cucumber and mix with 1 tablespoon **salt.** Let stand for 20 to 30 minutes. Rinse; squeeze out water. Soak 4 small **Oriental dried mushrooms** in warm water to cover for about 30 minutes. Drain. Cut off and discard stems; squeeze caps dry and cut into thin slices.

In a bowl, combine 6 tablespoons **rice vinegar,** 2 tablespoons **sugar,** and ½ teaspoon *each* **soy sauce** and minced **fresh ginger;** stir until sugar is dissolved. Mix in cucumbers, mushrooms, and ¼ pound **small cooked shrimp.** Cover and refrigerate, stirring occasionally, for at least 30 minutes. Drain before assembling bundles.

Ice-cold Tofu Salad

Light and nutritious, this stylish salad makes a refreshing first course or lunch entrée. A subtle sweet-and-sour dressing flavors iced squares of tofu and shredded daikon.

Lemon-Soy Dressing (recipe follows)
1 package (1 lb. 5 oz.) regular tofu (bean curd)
5 cups ice cubes
3 cups water
1 piece daikon, about 3 inches long and 1½ to 2 inches in diameter, peeled and finely shredded
About 6 green onion tops
6 crushed red pepper flakes

Prepare Lemon-Soy Dressing; set aside.

Drain tofu. Cut block into 18 pieces, each about 1 by 1¼ inches. Place ice and water in a large bowl; add tofu. Cover and refrigerate for at least 30 minutes or until next day.

Squeeze daikon dry. Cut onion tops into twelve 1½-inch-long pieces and six 2¼-inch-long pieces.

Mound an equal portion of daikon on one side of each of 6 plates. Make a tiny depression in each mound and fill with a pepper flake. At the edge of each mound, arrange 1 long and 2 short pieces onion. Stagger 3 pieces of the tofu, side by side, in center of plates. Offer Lemon-Soy Dressing. Makes 6 servings.

Lemon-Soy Dressing. In a small pan, combine ⅓ cup *each* **lemon juice** and **soy sauce,** 5 teaspoons *each* **rice vinegar** and **mirin,** and ⅔ cup **dried bonito flakes** (*katsuobushi*). Bring to a boil over medium-high heat. Remove from heat; let cool, then cover and refrigerate until cold. Pour through a wire strainer lined with 3 layers of cheesecloth; discard bonito. If made ahead, cover and refrigerate for up to 1 week.

The Cooking of
Korea

Though influenced by elements of Chinese and Japanese cuisine, Korean cooking maintains its own distinct style. The country's cool northern climate has helped to shape a cuisine that's characterized by hearty, rib-sticking dishes; warming soups, a fondness for beef, and bold seasonings of soy, sesame, and hot red pepper all typify Korean cooking.

No authentic Korean meal is complete without kim chee, a pungent, fiery-hot combination of pickled vegetables. You may want to try making your own (see page 65). For those who prefer somewhat less assertive vegetable side dishes, we offer several alternatives to kim chee.

Rice, served plain or in combination with other ingredients (see page 64), is another staple food. Koreans prefer short-grain rice over the long-grain varieties more familiar to many Westerners; cook it as directed for Steamed Short-grain Rice, page 44.

Korean meals usually end simply, with a cup of tea (ginseng tea is especially prized). But after a special meal, fresh fruits may be served—apples, pears, persimmons, oranges, or plums. With the fruit, you may want to offer plain butter cookies, though they aren't a traditional Korean accompaniment.

Appetizers

Beef Tartare with Pear

The Korean version of steak tartare is an intriguing variation on the classic dish. Called *yuk hai*, it combines beef, vegetables, and sweet fresh pear.

- 1½ teaspoons crushed toasted sesame seeds (directions follow)
- 4 teaspoons soy sauce
- 2 teaspoons sugar
- 1 teaspoon minced fresh ginger
- ½ teaspoon minced or pressed garlic
- 2 tablespoons thinly sliced green onion (including top)
- ⅛ to ¼ teaspoon ground red pepper (cayenne)
- ½ pound lean boneless beef (sirloin or top round)
- 1 small, firm, ripe pear
  Lemon juice
  Butter or leaf lettuce leaves
- 4 egg yolks
- ¾ cup *each* finely shredded cabbage and carrot
  Korean hot red pepper paste (optional)

Prepare sesame seeds; place in a bowl and add soy, sugar, ginger, garlic, onion and pepper. Set aside.

Trim and discard fat from beef. Cut meat across the grain into ¼-inch-thick slices; then cut slices into matchstick pieces. Add beef to soy mixture; stir. (At this point, you may cover and refrigerate for up to 4 hours.)

Peel pear and cut into matchstick pieces; moisten with lemon juice. Line 4 salad plates with lettuce; mound a fourth of the meat mixture on each plate. Make a well in center of each portion; place 1 egg yolk in each well. Arrange pear, cabbage, and carrot around meat. Add a dab of pepper paste, if desired. To eat, mix meat with egg yolk; accompany each bite with pear and vegetables. Makes 4 servings.

Crushed toasted sesame seeds. In a wide frying pan over medium heat, toast ½ cup **sesame seeds,** shaking pan frequently, until golden (about 2 minutes). Transfer to a mortar or blender. Crush with pestle until coarsely crushed, or whirl very briefly in blender. Store airtight at room temperature for up to 3 weeks. Makes about ½ cup.

Korean women look with satisfaction at crocks of pungent, fermenting kim chee; hot red peppers dry atop the crocks.

 # Soups

Daikon Soup

Serve this simple soup before the meal, or in the Korean manner—at meal's end, thickened with rice.

4 cups regular-strength beef broth
1 clove garlic, minced or pressed
2 teaspoons soy sauce
1 teaspoon sesame oil
2 cups thinly sliced peeled daikon
Thinly sliced green onions (including tops)

In a 3-quart pan, combine broth, garlic, soy, and oil. Bring to a boil over high heat. Add daikon; cover, reduce heat, and simmer until tender to bite (10 to 15 minutes). Garnish with onions. Makes 6 cups.

Korean Dumpling Soup

Purchased wrappers streamline preparation of this classic Korean soup, *mandoo*.

¼ cup crushed toasted sesame seeds (page 61)
Water
2 cups bean sprouts
1 tablespoon salad oil
½ pound *each* lean ground beef and firm tofu
2 cloves garlic, minced or pressed
½ cup sliced green onions (including tops)
2 tablespoons soy sauce
Pepper
½ pound won ton skins (about 40)
6 cups regular-strength beef broth

Prepare sesame seeds; set aside. Half-fill a 2 to 3-quart pan with water. Bring to a boil over high heat; add bean sprouts and cook just until boil resumes. Drain sprouts, then chop and squeeze dry.

Heat oil in a wide frying pan over medium-high heat. Crumble in beef; cook, stirring, until no longer pink. Remove from heat; stir in 2 tablespoons of the sesame seeds, sprouts, tofu, garlic, ¼ cup of the onions, and soy. Season to taste with pepper.

To make each dumpling, place 1½ teaspoons filling in center of a won ton skin. Moisten edges and fold in half to form a triangle; pinch edges to seal. Keep covered while filling remaining skins.

Pour broth and 2 cups water into a 5 to 6-quart kettle; bring to a boil over high heat. Add about a third of the dumplings; reduce heat and cook until skins are tender to bite (2 to 3 minutes). Lift out with a slotted spoon; set aside. Repeat with remaining dumplings. Return dumplings to kettle; add remaining sesame seeds and onions. Makes 6 servings.

Whole-meal Rib Soup
(Pictured on facing page)

In this hearty soup, *kalbi gook*, meaty short ribs are made tender by long, gentle cooking.

2 tablespoons crushed toasted sesame seeds (page 61)
2 pounds lean beef short ribs, cut into 2 to 3-inch lengths
3 cups regular-strength beef broth
6 cups water
⅓ cup soy sauce
3 tablespoons sugar
2 teaspoons minced or pressed garlic
3 quarter-size slices fresh ginger
½ to ¾ teaspoon ground red pepper (cayenne)
4 whole green onions, tied in a bundle
¼ pound daikon, peeled and thinly sliced
1 tablespoon sesame oil
3 or 4 eggs
Thinly sliced green onions (including tops)

Prepare sesame seeds; place in a 5 to 6-quart kettle and add ribs, broth, water, soy, sugar, garlic, ginger, pepper, and whole onions. Bring to a boil over medium heat; cover, reduce heat, and simmer until beef is tender when pierced (2½ to 3 hours).

With a slotted spoon, lift out ribs; let cool. Lift out and discard ginger and onions. Skim and discard fat from broth. When ribs are cool, discard bones and excess fat; then shred meat with your fingers. Return meat to broth and add daikon. Bring to a boil over medium-high heat; then cover, reduce heat, and simmer until daikon is tender to bite (10 to 15 minutes). Add oil. Gently break eggs, one at a time, into barely simmering broth; cover and cook just until eggs are softly set (about 2 minutes).

Ladle soup and eggs into individual bowls; sprinkle sliced onions over top. Makes 3 or 4 servings.

Whole-meal Rib Soup *(Recipe on facing page)*

1 Toast sesame seeds until golden to bring out their nutty flavor.

2 After removing cooked ribs from broth, skim and discard fat floating on top of broth.

3 Fingers make fast work of shredding meat from ribs trimmed of bones and fat.

4 Crack each egg and drop directly into kettle of simmering broth; cook just until softly set.

The Cooking of Korea   63

 # Rice & Vegetables

Rice & Bean Sprouts

You could call this a simplified fried rice. A quick and delicious side dish, it's crunchy and boldly flavored with the characteristic Korean seasonings of soy and sesame.

> 3 tablespoons crushed toasted sesame seeds (page 61)
> 1 tablespoon salad oil
> 2 green onions (including tops), minced
> 1 clove garlic, minced or pressed
> 1½ cups bean sprouts
> 2 cups hot Steamed Short-grain Rice (page 44)
> 2 tablespoons soy sauce

Prepare sesame seeds. Heat oil in a wide frying pan over medium heat. Then add sesame seeds, onions, and garlic; cook, stirring, until onions are soft. Add bean sprouts and cook, stirring, just until heated through.

Add rice and soy and mix gently, being careful not to mash rice grains. Makes about 4 servings.

Steamed Rice in Seaweed

This popular Korean rice dish is similar to Japanese sushi. Squares of dried seaweed (called *nori* in Japanese, *kim* in Korean) are toasted and topped with rice, then folded up and eaten out of hand.

> **Steamed Short-grain Rice (page 44)**
> **Roasted or unroasted nori**
> **Soy sauce**

Prepare rice, allowing ½ to 1 cup cooked rice per person. Toast nori as directed on page 43, allowing about ¼ ounce per person. With scissors, cut toasted nori into 4 to 5-inch squares.

Spoon hot rice into nori. Sprinkle lightly with soy; fold to enclose and eat out of hand. Or place hot rice in small individual bowls; top with bits of crumbled nori and soy to taste.

Seoul Green Beans

Green beans and mushrooms, deftly seasoned with a dash of sesame oil and a hint of pepper, are a sprightly accompaniment to Oriental and occidental entrées alike.

> 1 pound green beans, ends removed
> 10 large mushrooms, thinly sliced
> ¾ cup boiling water
> ⅛ to ¼ teaspoon pepper
> Soy sauce or salt
> 1 tablespoon sesame oil

Cut beans lengthwise into thin slivers. Place beans and mushrooms in a 3 to 4-quart pan; then pour in water and place pan over medium-high heat. Cover and cook until beans are tender to bite (6 to 8 minutes). Immediately remove from heat; drain well.

Sprinkle bean mixture with pepper and season to taste with soy, then drizzle with oil. Toss to distribute seasonings; spoon into a warm serving dish. Makes 4 servings.

Marinated Vegetables
(Pictured on page 71)

Simple to make and refreshing to eat is *namul:* raw or briefly cooked vegetables (carrots, bean sprouts, spinach, or watercress) tossed with an easy soy-sesame dressing just before serving. Serve namul in the Korean manner—with the entrée—or offer it as a light first course.

> **Prepared vegetable (directions follow)**
> 3 teaspoons crushed toasted sesame seeds (page 61)
> 1 tablespoon soy sauce
> 2 teaspoons *each* sesame oil and minced green onion (including top)
> 1 teaspoon *each* sugar and vinegar
> ¹⁄₁₆ to ⅛ teaspoon ground red pepper (cayenne)

Prepare your choice of vegetable; if cooked, let cool to room temperature.

Prepare sesame seeds. Place 2 teaspoons of the seeds in a small bowl; then stir in soy, oil, onion, sugar, vinegar, and pepper. Combine sesame-soy mixture with prepared vegetable. Sprinkle with remaining 1 teaspoon sesame seeds and serve immediately. Makes 4 servings.

Bean sprouts. Half-fill a 5-quart kettle with water and bring to a boil over high heat. Add ¾ pound **bean sprouts** and cook just until boil resumes; drain.

Carrots. Cut 5 or 6 large **carrots** into matchstick pieces (you should have about 3 cups). Place a steaming rack in a wide frying pan; then pour in water to a depth of 1 inch and bring to a boil over high heat. Arrange carrots on rack; steam, covered, until tender-crisp to bite (about 5 minutes).

Spinach. Remove and discard tough stems from 3 pounds **spinach.** Rinse thoroughly, but do not dry. Place about a third of spinach (with water that clings to leaves) in a wide frying pan. Place over high heat and cook, stirring occasionally, until spinach is wilted (about 1 minute). Squeeze out excess liquid. Repeat with remaining spinach.

Watercress. Discard tough stems from 1 large bunch **watercress** (about 2½ cups). Rinse; pat dry. If desired, omit pepper from dressing.

Seasoned Cucumbers

This crisp and chunky condiment complements soy-seasoned meats. Though piquant, it's milder than most versions of *kim chee.*

  2 **large cucumbers**
  2 **teaspoons salt**
  1 **green onion (including top), thinly sliced**
  1 **clove garlic, minced or pressed**
  ½ **teaspoon *each* sugar and minced fresh ginger**
  ¼ **to ½ teaspoon Korean red pepper or ground red pepper (cayenne)**

Score cucumbers, if desired; then cut in half lengthwise. Scoop out and discard seeds. Cut halves lengthwise to make quarters; cut each quarter crosswise into 1-inch pieces. Place in a large bowl with salt; mix well and let stand at room temperature for 15 minutes. Rinse well and drain; return to bowl along with onion, garlic, sugar, ginger, and pepper. Cover and refrigerate for at least 4 hours or until next day. Makes about 3 cups.

Kim Chee

Mention the phrase "Korean food" and nine out of ten who have sampled it will remember, if nothing else, the *kim chee.* And understandably so, for this dish of hot and pungent pickled vegetables is basic to Korean cooking (in fact, it's served at every meal—even breakfast).

In Korea, kim chee is traditionally made in autumn, in batches large enough to last a family through the following winter and spring. The spicy cabbage mixture is packed in large crocks (like those pictured on page 60), then allowed to ferment.

You'll find kim chee sold in Oriental markets and some supermarkets. Hotness and pungency vary from brand to brand, but most are quite potent—one good reason to consider making your own. By controlling the degree of fermentation and adjusting the amount of red pepper, you can make homemade kim chee as mild or bold as you like.

Our cabbage kim chee is authentically hot if you use the maximum amount of red pepper. Strips of daikon make a slightly more pungent pickle; omit them if you prefer a milder version.

Cabbage Pickles with Daikon

  1 **medium-size head napa cabbage (1½ to 2 lbs.)**
  2½ **tablespoons salt**
  ¼ **pound daikon, peeled and cut into matchstick pieces (optional)**
  2 **green onions (including tops), cut into thin slivers**
  3 **cloves garlic, minced or pressed**
  1 **to 2 teaspoons Korean red pepper or ground red pepper (cayenne)**
  2 **teaspoons sugar**

Cut cabbage into chunks about 1 inch square; place in a large bowl and add 2 tablespoons of the salt. Mix well. Cover and let stand at room temperature until cabbage is wilted and reduced to about half its original volume (3 to 4 hours). Rinse thoroughly; drain. Return to bowl along with daikon (if used), onions, garlic, pepper, sugar, and remaining ½ tablespoon salt; mix well. Pack lightly into a 1-quart jar; cover with lid or plastic wrap and let stand at room temperature, tasting often, until fermented to your liking. (In warm weather, fermentation may take only 1 to 2 days; in cooler weather, count on 3 to 4 days.) Store in the refrigerator, covered, for up to 2 weeks. Makes about 3½ cups.

Chicken with Four Colored Vegetables *(Recipe on facing page)*

1 Cut chicken with the grain into 1½-inch strips, then slice each strip thinly across the grain.

2 Snip and discard tough stems from soaked mushrooms; slice caps.

3 Drain soaked bean threads; then cut them into easy-to-eat 4-inch lengths.

4 Noodles soak up flavorful pan juices as they heat through. Toss to distribute juices evenly.

Chicken

Chicken with Four Colored Vegetables

(Pictured on facing page)

This traditional Korean dish makes a pretty lunch or dinner entrée. Strips of chicken breast and the four colored vegetables—brown mushrooms, white onions, orange carrots, and green beans—are stir-fried, then arranged atop briefly cooked noodles and tossed at the table.

  About ½ cup crushed toasted sesame seeds (page 61)
1½ pounds chicken breasts, skinned and boned
  Soy sauce
  6 green onions (including tops)
  1 ounce Oriental dried mushrooms
  8 ounces bean threads
  3 small carrots
  ⅓ pound green beans, ends removed
  5 tablespoons salad oil
  2 cloves garlic, minced or pressed
  ¼ teaspoon *each* sugar and pepper

Prepare sesame seeds; set aside. Cut chicken with the grain into 1½-inch-wide strips. Then cut each strip across the grain into slices about ⅛ inch thick. (Chicken is easier to cut if it's partially frozen.) Place chicken in a bowl with 1 teaspoon soy. Mince white part only of 1 of the onions; add to chicken. Stir and set aside. Slice onion top; reserve for garnish.

Soak mushrooms in warm water to cover for about 30 minutes. Cut off and discard stems; cut caps into ½-inch-wide strips. Also soak bean threads in warm water to cover for about 30 minutes; drain, cut into 4-inch lengths, and set aside.

Cut carrots diagonally into ⅛-inch-thick slices. Slice beans and remaining 5 onions into pieces about the same size as carrot slices.

Heat 1 tablespoon of the oil in a wok or wide frying pan over medium-high heat. Add onions and mushrooms and cook, stirring, for 1 minute; remove from pan and set aside. Add 1 more tablespoon oil to pan; then add carrots and beans and cook, stirring, for 5 minutes. Add garlic, sugar, pepper, 1 tablespoon of the sesame seeds, and 3 tablespoons soy. Return onions and mushrooms to pan and cook, stirring, until carrots are tender-crisp to bite (about 3 more minutes). Remove and set aside.

Add 1 more tablespoon oil to pan; add chicken and cook, stirring, until chicken is opaque throughout (about 3 minutes). Stir in 1 more tablespoon soy. With a slotted spoon, transfer chicken to a small bowl, leaving any juices in pan. Add remaining 2 tablespoons oil and bean threads to pan and stir until noodles are heated through and pan juices are absorbed. Transfer to a wide, shallow serving bowl.

Mound chicken atop noodles; arrange vegetables around chicken. Sprinkle with 1 more tablespoon soy, another tablespoon of the sesame seeds, and reserved sliced onion top. Serve at room temperature. Toss at the table; pass additional soy and remaining sesame seeds to sprinkle over individual servings. Makes about 4 servings.

Crunchy Chicken Salad

Moist and tender chicken combines with a colorful variety of crisp, raw vegetables in this salad. It's a good candidate for a lunch entrée.

  2 tablespoons crushed toasted sesame seeds (page 61)
  Mustard-Soy Dressing (recipe follows)
3½ to 4 cups shredded cooked chicken
  2 cups finely shredded iceberg lettuce
  1 cup *each* matchstick strips carrot and cucumber
  ⅔ cup thin 2-inch-long strips green onions (including tops)
  1 cup bean sprouts
  ¾ cup roasted salted almonds
  Salt and pepper

Prepare sesame seeds; set aside.

Prepare Mustard-Soy Dressing. In a large salad bowl, combine chicken, lettuce, carrot, cucumber, onions, bean sprouts, ½ cup of the almonds, and sesame seeds. Add dressing (stir first); mix gently. Season to taste with salt and pepper; top with remaining ¼ cup almonds. Makes 4 to 6 servings.

Mustard-Soy Dressing. In a small bowl, stir together ¼ teaspoon *each* **dry mustard** and **liquid hot pepper seasoning**; 1½ teaspoons **soy sauce**; 2 tablespoons **salad oil**; 1 tablespoon **sesame oil**; and 2 teaspoons **lemon juice.**

 **Meats**

Korean Hot Pot

Sin sul lo, usually served on special occasions in Korea, could be just the right main course for your next small dinner party. The traditional cooking pot—also called sin sul lo—is a brass bowl with a pedestal base; a chimney in its center holds burning charcoal to keep foods in the bowl hot. (See page 101 for alternate cooking equipment.) Guests help themselves to meat and vegetables from the pot, then sip broth from bowls afterwards.

> ¼ cup *each* **crushed toasted sesame seeds (page 61) and soy sauce**
> 1 **clove garlic, minced or pressed**
> 2 **tablespoons salad oil**
> 1 **pound lean boneless beef (sirloin or top round), thinly sliced across the grain**
> 1 **pound ground pork**
> About 2 **tablespoons pine nuts or about ¼ cup walnut pieces**
> 1 **pound spinach, rinsed well**
> ½ **teaspoon salt**
> 2 **eggs**
> **All-purpose flour**
> **Salad oil**
> ¼ **pound mushrooms, thinly sliced**
> 2 *each* **medium-size carrots and turnips**
> **Garnishes (suggestions follow)**
> 8 **cups regular-strength beef broth**
> **Hot cooked rice (optional)**

Prepare sesame seeds. Place in a large bowl; add soy, garlic, and the 2 tablespoons oil. Mix well.

Cut beef slices into 2 to 3-inch-wide strips (if you're using a hot pot, cut slices the width of the moat). Place in a bowl; stir in half the sesame-soy mixture. Set aside. Combine pork with remaining sesame-soy mixture. Form into small balls (½ to ¾ inch in diameter), inserting a pine nut in middle of each; set aside.

Remove stems from spinach. Into a 2 to 3-quart pan, pour water to a depth of 1 inch. Bring to a boil; add salt. Gently push spinach down into water. Cook and stir just until limp (about 30 seconds); drain. Let cool slightly; then gently press out excess liquid. Carefully stack leaves to make piles about ½ inch thick. In a small bowl, lightly beat eggs. Dredge spinach stacks in flour; shake off excess and dip stacks in egg. Pour enough oil into a wide frying pan to coat bottom; place over medium-high heat. Cook stacks until lightly browned on both sides (about 3 minutes per side); remove from pan and cut crosswise into 1-inch slices. Set aside. Add more oil to pan (if needed) to coat bottom. Dredge pork balls in flour; shake off excess. Dip in egg; then cook, a few at a time, until browned on all sides. Set aside.

Heat 1½ teaspoons oil in a small pan over medium-high heat. Add mushrooms and cook, stirring, until lightly browned; set aside.

In a 2 to 3-quart pan, bring 1 inch water to a boil over high heat. Add carrots; reduce heat to medium and cook just until tender when pierced (8 to 10 minutes). Drain and set aside. Into pan, pour water to a depth of 2 inches and bring to a boil over high heat. Add turnips; reduce heat to medium and cook until tender when pierced (about 15 minutes). Score carrots lengthwise, making 4 equally spaced ¼-inch-deep cuts; then cut into thin slices (they'll look like small flowers). Cut turnips into ¼-inch-thick slices; cut slices into ¼-inch-wide strips.

Place half of each ingredient in a separate mound in hot pot (or other pan), in this order: turnips, beef, carrots, spinach, pork balls. Repeat with remaining ingredients, to fill pot. Arrange your choice of garnishes on top.

Set cooking pot in middle of table. Pour broth into a 3 to 4-quart pan. Heat over high heat until steaming; pour into pot. (If you're using a hot pot, half-fill chimney with glowing charcoal at this point.) Cover and simmer until meat and vegetables are heated through; uncover and let diners serve themselves. After meat and vegetables have been eaten, ladle broth into soup bowls (add a spoonful of rice to each, if desired). Makes 4 to 6 servings.

Garnishes. Choose at least 3 of the following: Sliced **hard-cooked eggs,** sliced **green onions** (including tops), shelled **walnuts** or pistachios, sliced **steamed fishcakes** (*kamaboko*), **mushroom or spinach slices** or **pork balls** reserved from cooking ingredients.

Beef & Watercress in Egg Batter

These little patties, called *minari juhn*, are a cross between a savory pancake and egg foo yung. Tender morsels of meat and lively vegetables cooked in an egg-based batter are just right for a light lunch or supper entrée. Serve as finger food—or, to serve Korean style, provide each diner with a bowl of rice and a small bowl of dipping sauce. Place a pancake on rice and break off bits with chopsticks; then dip into sauce.

>**Sesame Dipping Sauce (recipe follows)**
> 3 tablespoons *each* all-purpose flour and water
> 3 eggs
> ½ pound lean boneless beef (sirloin, top round, or flank)
> 1¼ cups coarsely chopped, lightly packed watercress leaves and small stems
> ¼ cup thinly sliced green onions (including tops)
> ¼ teaspoon salt
> ⅛ teaspoon pepper
> **About 2 tablespoons salad oil**

Prepare Sesame Dipping Sauce; set aside.

In a medium-size bowl, mix flour and water until smooth. Add eggs and beat to blend. Thinly slice beef across the grain; then cut slices into bite-size pieces. Add to egg mixture along with watercress, onions, salt, and pepper. Mix gently but thoroughly.

Heat 2 tablespoons of the oil in a wide frying pan over medium heat. Dip out about a tablespoon of the meat mixture, being sure to include some of the egg batter in each spoonful; place in pan, forming a small patty (you can cook 4 or 5 at a time). Cook patties until lightly browned on both sides (about 3 minutes per side); then keep warm in a 200° oven. Repeat until all meat mixture has been used, adding more oil to pan as necessary. Serve with Sesame Dipping Sauce. Makes about 25 patties (3 or 4 servings).

Sesame Dipping Sauce. In a small bowl, stir together 3 tablespoons **soy sauce,** 2 tablespoons **rice vinegar,** 1 tablespoon **sesame oil,** 1 teaspoon **crushed toasted sesame seeds** (page 61), and ⅛ to ¼ teaspoon **crushed red pepper.** Serve in small individual bowls.

Pork & Spinach in Egg Batter

Follow directions for **Beef & Watercress in Egg Batter,** substituting ½ pound **lean boneless pork** (butt or leg), cut into bite-size pieces, for beef. Also substitute ⅓ pound **spinach,** well rinsed, coarse stems removed, and leaves coarsely chopped, for watercress. Serve with Sesame Dipping Sauce.

Fried Beef Liver

The Korean term *jun* covers a category of dishes that share a common method of cooking. Thin slices of liver or fish are dipped in flour, then in egg; then they're briefly fried and served piping hot.

>**Sesame Dipping Sauce (optional; this page)**
> 1 pound baby beef liver, cut into ½-inch-thick slices, membranes removed
> 2 tablespoons soy sauce
> 1 green onion (including top), minced
> 2 cloves garlic, minced or pressed
> **Pepper**
> ⅔ cup all-purpose flour
> 3 eggs
> **Salad oil**

Prepare Sesame Dipping Sauce, if desired; set aside. Cut liver into ½-inch-wide strips. In a bowl, combine soy, onion, and garlic; season to taste with pepper. Add liver and stir to mix. Place flour in a pie pan. In a small bowl, lightly beat eggs.

Into a wide frying pan, pour oil to a depth of about ¼ inch; heat over medium-high heat until a pinch of flour floats and sizzles when dropped on oil. Lift liver from marinade and drain briefly. Dredge in flour, shake off excess, and dip in egg. Place a few pieces of liver in pan and cook until browned; drain briefly on paper towels. Keep warm in a 200° oven. Repeat with remaining liver. If desired, serve with dipping sauce. Makes 4 servings.

Fried Fish Squares

Cut 1 pound **sole fillets** (*each* about ½ inch thick) into 2-inch-square pieces. Season to taste with **salt** and **pepper.** Dredge in flour and egg and cook as directed for **Fried Beef Liver,** using only ⅛ inch of oil in pan. Serve with Sesame Dipping Sauce. Makes 4 servings.

Barbecued Short Ribs
(Pictured on front cover)

When you're in the mood for finger food, try *kalbi.* Before cooking, chunky short ribs are scored in a crosshatched pattern; the scoring makes it easy for flavors from the marinade and heat from the barbecue to penetrate the meat. (Or butterfly ribs into a long, flat, quick-cooking strip.)

(Continued on next page)

⅓ cup crushed toasted sesame seeds (page 61)

4 pounds lean beef short ribs, cut into 2½-inch lengths

1 cup soy sauce

⅓ cup sugar

2½ tablespoons *each* minced garlic and fresh ginger

⅓ cup sesame oil

⅔ cup thinly sliced green onions (including tops)

Prepare sesame seeds; set aside.

Place ribs, bone side down, on cutting board. Make a series of parallel cuts ½ inch apart, cutting halfway to bone each time. Then make another series of parallel cuts at right angles to the first set; space cuts ½ inch apart and cut ½ inch deep each time. In a bowl, combine sesame seeds, soy, sugar, garlic, ginger, oil, and onions. Combine meat with soy mixture. Cover and refrigerate for about 4 hours.

Place ribs on a lightly greased grill 4 to 6 inches above a solid bed of glowing coals. Cook until browned on all sides and done to your liking when slashed (15 to 20 minutes for medium-rare). Makes 4 to 6 servings.

Note: You may also use 3½ to 4-inch-long ribs. Score, marinate, and cook as directed above (cook for about 20 minutes). To serve, cut meat off bones. Eat with knife and fork.

Butterflied Short Ribs

You'll need 4 pounds **lean beef short ribs,** cut into 2 to 3-inch lengths. Butterfly-cut ribs, one piece at a time. First, set rib on its side. Then, starting about ¼ inch from bone, cut to within ¼ inch of end of piece. Turn rib and make a parallel cut in opposite direction about ¼ inch from first cut. Continue cutting in this way until you can spread meat out in a long, flat strip. Marinate and cook as directed for **Barbecued Short Ribs,** cooking until browned on both sides (5 to 10 minutes *total*). Makes 4 to 6 servings.

Barbecued Beef Strips

(Pictured on facing page)

Tender slices of beef, flavored in a soy-sesame marinade, form the base for several Korean dishes. You barbecue the meat to make *bul gogi;* stir-fried, it's called *gogi bokum.* For *sang chi sam,* the stir-fried beef is combined with rice and served in lettuce cups.

1 tablespoon crushed toasted sesame seeds (page 61)

1½ pounds lean boneless beef (sirloin, top round, or chuck)

6 tablespoons soy sauce

2 tablespoons *each* sugar and sesame oil

1 green onion (including top), thinly sliced

2 cloves garlic, minced or pressed

1 teaspoon grated fresh ginger
   Dash of pepper

Prepare sesame seeds; set aside.

Cut meat across the grain into thin slices (about ⅛ inch thick). In a bowl, stir together sesame seeds, soy, sugar, oil, onion, garlic, ginger, and pepper. Combine meat with soy mixture; cover and refrigerate for 1 to 1½ hours.

To cook, place meat on a lightly greased grill about 4 inches above a solid bed of glowing coals. Cook, turning once, just until browned on both sides (2 to 3 minutes *total*). Serve immediately. Makes 4 to 6 servings.

Stir-fried Beef Strips

Cut and marinate beef as directed for **Barbecued Beef Strips.**

To cook, place a wok or wide frying pan over high heat and add 2 tablespoons **salad oil.** When oil is hot, add about half the meat mixture and 1 to 2 tablespoons of the marinade. Cook, stirring constantly, just until meat is browned on both sides (2 to 3 minutes *total*). Remove from pan; keep warm. Cook remaining beef, adding more oil (if needed) and 1 to 2 more tablespoons marinade. Serve immediately. Makes 4 to 6 servings.

Beef & Rice in Lettuce

Cut beef as directed for **Barbecued Beef Strips,** but use only 1 pound. In a bowl, stir together 2½ tablespoons **soy sauce,** 1 tablespoon *each* **sugar, sesame oil,** and **crushed toasted sesame seeds** (page 61), 1 teaspoon *each* minced **garlic** and **fresh ginger,** and 2 tablespoons thinly sliced **green onion** (including top). Mix beef with soy mixture. Cook as directed for **Stir-fried Beef Strips.**

On each of 4 dinner plates, arrange about a fourth of the beef, about ½ cup **Steamed Short-grain Rice** (page 44), 5 to 8 **red leaf lettuce leaves,** and, if desired, a dab of **Korean hot red pepper paste.**

To eat, fill a lettuce leaf with meat, rice, and pepper paste (if used). Roll up and eat out of hand. Makes 4 servings.

Barbecued Beef Strips *(Recipe on facing page)* with Marinated Vegetables *(recipe on page 64)*

1 Cut lean beef across the grain into long, thin slices (about ⅛ inch thick).

2 Combine beef strips with soy-sesame marinade; mix thoroughly with chopsticks or spoon.

3 Beef cooks quickly over small barbecue. Serve immediately, then grill the next batch.

The Cooking of Korea   71

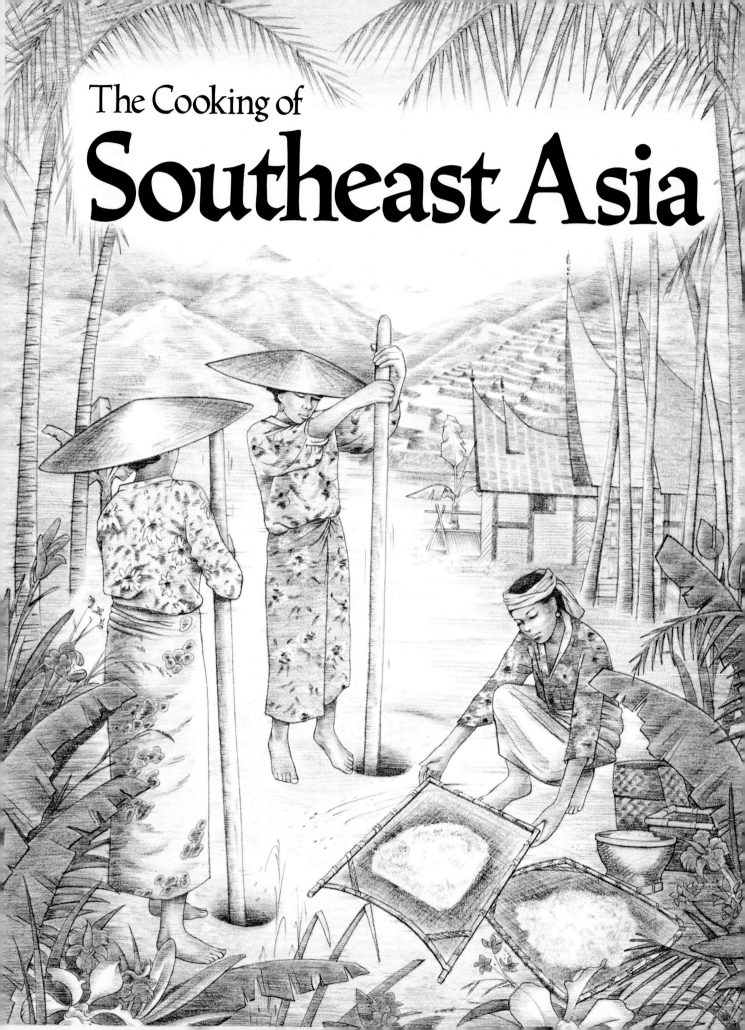

The Cooking of
Southeast Asia

Southeast Asia is a feast for the senses—ornate pagodas, green mountainsides terraced for farming, colorful outdoor markets, and roadside food stalls. Even if you haven't traveled to these exotic lands, you can still experience the flavor of the region through its cooking.

Southeast Asia stretches more than 3,000 miles, encompassing nine countries—Burma, Thailand, Vietnam, Laos, Cambodia (Kampuchea), Malaysia, Singapore, Indonesia, and the Philippines. Geographically and culturally, this is one of the world's most diverse regions.

The cuisines of its member nations are equally diverse, but linked by the use of common ingredients: tart and fruity tamarind, lemon grass, chiles, fish sauce, coconut milk, sweet spices, and gingery galangal. Certain dishes, too, could be called typically Southeast Asian. These include curries of meat or fish in coconut milk, well-seasoned rice and noodle dishes, and satay: skewered, grilled bits of meat.

Certain ingredients are most characteristic of particular countries. For example, sweet spices—cinnamon, cloves, cardamom, anise—are used liberally in the cooking of Indonesia and Malaysia, whose ports were once stopping points along the China-India spice trade route.

Though Indochinese cooking has its share of spicy-hot dishes, the cuisines of Vietnam, Laos, and Cambodia also share a lighter touch, a blending of more subtle flavors. An important seasoning here is a pungent fish sauce added (in small amounts) to many dishes. (We've used milder Thai fish sauce in most recipes.)

Through trade, immigration, invasion, and colonization, Southeast Asia has long been subject to foreign influence. No wonder, then, that the successful blending of native and foreign elements is a hallmark of the region's cuisine. The Dutch have left their mark in Indonesia, the French in Vietnam, the English in Singapore. European influences are especially apparent in the Philippines, which were governed by Spain for over 300 years. Filipinos tend to prefer slower cooking methods such as braising to the stir-frying typical of Asia.

In Southeast Asia, as in all of Asia, rice is the staple grain, served with every meal. Rice is also made into noodles and pressed into transparent, papery wrappers for savory fillings.

With Southeast Asian restaurants springing up all over the United States, more diners are discovering the region's cuisines. And since typical ingredients are now easier to find, you can create the dishes of the tropics in your own kitchen.

Women process rice after the harvest, first pounding the kernels, then winnowing chaff from the grain.

Imperial Rolls

(Recipe on facing page)

1 Brush curling edges of rice paper lightly with water so round will lie flat; place on wire rack until pliable.

2 Tuck sides around filling in two stages. First, fold right and left edges in at a 45° angle to the horizontal.

3 Brush folded-in edges of rice paper generously with egg white to seal.

4 Second fold forms a straight-sided edge, ready to roll and seal.

 # Appetizers

Imperial Rolls
(Pictured on facing page)

These Vietnamese delicacies may look like egg rolls, but they differ in several ways. The most notable difference is in the wrapper: for imperial rolls, you use tissue-thin rice paper.

> Pork & Shrimp Filling (recipe follows)
> Dipping Sauce (page 92)
> About 12 rice paper rounds, each about 8½ inches in diameter
> Beer or water
> 1 egg white
> Salad oil
> About 36 butter lettuce leaves (optional)
> Fresh mint leaves (optional)

Prepare filling and Dipping Sauce; set aside.

With your hands or a pastry brush, lightly moisten both sides of rice paper rounds (2 or 3 at a time) with beer or water; place on a wire rack and let stand until pliable (2 to 3 minutes). Keep remaining papers in package until you're ready to use them.

To fill and roll each paper, first place 2 tablespoons of the filling in a 3-inch-long strip across paper about 2 inches above bottom. Fold bottom edge over filling; roll once to enclose. Fold in right and left edges of rolled portion of paper at a 45° angle to the horizontal; brush with egg white. Then fold sides of paper toward center, so folds are vertical; brush folded-in edges and top edge generously with egg white. Roll up, sealing top edge. Brush again with egg white. Continue to moisten, fill, and roll papers until all filling has been used, placing filled rolls in a single layer on a baking sheet.

Into a 3 to 4-quart pan, pour oil to a depth of 2 inches and heat to 300° on a deep-frying thermometer. Add 2 or 3 rolls and increase heat to 325°. Cook, turning occasionally, until crisp and light golden (about 6 minutes). Lift out and drain on paper towels. Serve immediately; or let cool, then cover and refrigerate until next day (or freeze for up to 4 weeks). To reheat, thaw if frozen; heat, uncovered, in a 350° oven for 10 minutes or until heated through.

To serve, cut each roll into thirds with a serrated knife. Place on a platter with a bowl of Dipping Sauce; dip rolls into sauce. Or, if desired, surround rolls with lettuce and mint leaves. To eat, place a mint leaf in a lettuce leaf; top with a roll piece, fold up, and dip into sauce. Makes about 36 appetizers.

Pork & Shrimp Filling. Soak 3 or 4 large **dried black fungus** in warm water to cover until soft (15 to 20 minutes). Pinch out and discard hard, knobby centers; cut remaining fungus into thin strips about 1 inch long. Set aside. Also soak 1 ounce **bean threads** in warm water to cover until soft (about 30 minutes). Drain and cut into 1-inch lengths. Set aside.

Heat 1 tablespoon **salad oil** in a wok or wide frying pan over high heat. Add ½ pound **ground pork** and ½ cup finely chopped **onion.** Cook, stirring, until pork is lightly browned (about 3 minutes). Add ¼ pound **medium-size shrimp,** peeled, deveined, and chopped, and 2 cloves **garlic,** minced or pressed; continue cooking until shrimp turns pink (about 2 more minutes).

Transfer to a large bowl and add 1 large **carrot,** shredded; 2½ teaspoons **sugar;** ½ teaspoon *each* **salt** and **pepper;** fungus; bean threads; and ¼ pound **bean sprouts,** cut into 1-inch pieces. Stir until well combined; let cool to room temperature.

Cucumbers with Tomato Relish

Cucumber spears serve as scoops for tomato relish in this appetizer treat from Burma.

> Tomato Relish (recipe follows)
> 2 large cucumbers

Prepare Tomato Relish. Peel cucumbers; cut lengthwise into sixths, then cut into 4-inch-long spears. Arrange on a platter around relish. Makes 10 servings.

Tomato Relish. In a blender or food processor, whirl until well minced: 2 to 4 **small dried whole hot red chiles,** stemmed and seeded; 2 tablespoons **water;** 1 large **onion,** cut into chunks; 4 cloves **garlic,** halved; and 2 teaspoons chopped **fresh ginger.** Heat 2 tablespoons **salad oil** in a wide frying pan over medium heat; add onion mixture and ¼ teaspoon **turmeric** and cook, stirring, until liquid has evaporated (about 5 minutes). Remove from heat. Drain 1 large can (28 oz.) **tomatoes;** whirl in blender until smooth. Add to onion mixture; season to taste with **salt.** Cook over medium heat, stirring, until reduced to about 2 cups. Serve at room temperature.

ข้าว Soups

Seafood Firepot

Aromatic, hot-tart soup, chock-full of fresh seafood, makes an eye-catching party entrée. It's like a Thai *cioppino*—but based on a citrus-scented clear broth instead of a garlicky tomato mixture.

- 12 cups regular-strength chicken broth
- 3 cups water
- 1 stalk fresh lemon grass or ¼ cup sliced dry lemon grass or yellow part of peel from 1 lemon
- 1 or 2 fresh or pickled hot chiles (*each* 2½ inches long), thinly sliced
  Green part of peel from 1 lime
- 18 small live hard-shell clams, scrubbed
- 1½ pounds large shrimp, shelled and deveined
  About 2 pounds cooked whole crab (such as Dungeness or blue), cleaned and cracked
- ⅔ cup lime juice
- ½ cup fresh coriander (cilantro) sprigs
- 3 green onions (including tops), cut into 1-inch lengths
  Lime wedges

In an 8 to 10-quart kettle, combine broth and water. Slice lemon grass. Loosely tie lemon grass, chiles (reserve 4 to 6 slices for garnish), and lime peel in a piece of moistened cheesecloth; add to kettle. Bring to a boil over high heat; cover, reduce heat, and simmer for 45 minutes..Discard seasonings.

Add clams, shrimp, and crab to kettle. Cover and simmer until clams open and shrimp turn pink (about 7 minutes). Stir in lime juice. Lift out seafood and place in a large serving bowl; pour in broth. Garnish with chile slices, coriander, and onions. Serve with lime wedges. Makes 4 to 6 servings.

Chicken Soup with Condiments

There are probably as many versions of *soto ayam* as there are cooks in Indonesia. In our rendition, chicken and condiments embellish a delicate broth.

- 1 frying chicken (3 to 3½ lbs.)
- 1 tablespoon salad oil
- 4 cloves garlic, smashed, then peeled
- 1 onion, coarsely chopped
- 2 tablespoons chopped fresh ginger
- 1 stalk fresh or dry lemon grass or ¼ cup sliced dry lemon grass or yellow part of peel from 1 lemon
- 1 slice dry galangal (optional)
- 1 teaspoon *each* turmeric and salt
- 2 teaspoons *each* ground coriander and sugar
- ¼ teaspoon pepper
- 2 cans (14½ oz. *each*) regular-strength chicken broth
- 4 cups water
  Condiments (suggestions follow)
  Crisp-fried Onions (recipe follows) or ⅓ cup sliced green onions (including tops)
- 1½ tablespoons lemon juice

Remove chicken giblets; set aside. Pull off and discard lumps of fat from chicken. Cut off wings and leg-and-thigh pieces; separate back from breast.

Pour oil into a 5 to 6-quart kettle and place over medium heat. Add garlic, onion, and ginger and cook, stirring, until onion is soft. Add lemon grass, galangal (if used), turmeric, salt, coriander, sugar, pepper, broth, and water; stir, then add chicken and giblets (except liver; reserve liver for other uses, if desired). Bring to a boil over high heat; cover, reduce heat, and simmer until breast is no longer pink when slashed (15 to 20 minutes).

Remove breast and let cool; simmer remaining chicken until meat near thighbone is no longer pink when slashed (15 more minutes). Lift out legs and thighs; let cool. Continue to simmer broth. Discard skin from breasts, legs, and thighs; cut meat into bite-size pieces. Cover and set aside.

Return bones to broth; continue simmering until broth is richly flavored (about 1 more hour). Strain, discarding wings, back, bones, giblets, and seasonings. (At this point, you may cover and refrigerate chicken and broth until next day. Bring chicken to room temperature before serving.)

Prepare condiments and Crisp-fried Onions. Place condiments, onions, and chicken in separate bowls. Skim and discard fat from broth; heat broth until steaming and stir in lemon juice. Ladle broth into bowls; let diners add chicken, condiments, and Crisp-fried Onions. Makes 6 to 8 servings.

Condiments. Offer at least 2 of the following: 2 ounces **bean threads,** cut into 6-inch lengths (soak in warm water to cover for 30 minutes before cutting), or 1½ cups cooked rice; 1½ cups **bean sprouts**

mixed with ¼ cup chopped **celery leaves; Spiced Coconut** (page 96); and **Chili Paste** (page 96).

Crisp-fried Onions. Cut 2 medium-size **onions** in half lengthwise. Cut each half crosswise into even slices about ⅛ inch thick; then cut slices into halves or thirds to make small arcs. Into a deep, heavy pan, pour **salad oil** to a depth of 1 inch and heat to 300° on a deep-frying thermometer. Add about a third of the onions and cook, stirring often, until lightly browned (4 to 5 minutes). Oil temperature will drop at first, but rise again as onions brown; regulate heat to maintain temperature at 300°. Remove onions with a slotted spoon; drain on paper towels. Repeat with remaining onions. Serve warm or at room temperature. Makes about 1½ cups.

Pork-Tofu Soup

Spinach, creamy tofu, and small meatballs combine in a seasoned broth to make a versatile soup. This Thai dish is a homey meal in a bowl all by itself (serve with rice, if you like); offered alongside the entrée, it lends a refreshing note to a spicy meal.

¾ **pound ground pork**
¼ **teaspoon pepper**
1 **tablespoon chopped fresh coriander (cilantro)**
1 **tablespoon fish sauce or soy sauce**
1 **tablespoon salad oil**
4 **cloves garlic, finely chopped**
1 **large can (49½ oz.) regular-strength chicken broth**
  About ¾ pound firm tofu (bean curd), cut into ½-inch cubes
1 **bunch spinach (about ¾ lb.), stems removed**
3 **green onions (including tops), cut into 1-inch lengths**

In a bowl, combine pork, pepper, coriander, and fish sauce. Mix until blended; then form into balls about ¾ inch in diameter and set aside.

Combine oil and garlic in a 4 to 5-quart kettle over medium-low heat. Cook, stirring, just until garlic is golden (about 10 minutes). Remove from kettle and set aside.

Add broth to kettle; bring to a boil over high heat. Reduce heat to medium and drop in meatballs. Add tofu; cover and simmer until meatballs are no longer pink when slashed (about 10 minutes). Skim and discard fat.

Meanwhile, rinse spinach well; cut leaves crosswise into 1-inch-wide strips. Add spinach and onions to soup. Cover and simmer until spinach is barely wilted (about 1 minute). Spoon garlic over soup. Makes 4 to 6 servings.

Sour Beef Soup

From Cambodia comes this thick, meaty soup, generously flavored with garlic and tamarind. Accompany the soup with rice or French bread, and you've got a whole meal.

1 **stalk fresh or dry lemon grass or ¼ cup sliced dry lemon grass or yellow part of peel from 1 lemon**
6 **slices dry galangal or 6 thin slices fresh ginger**
  About 3 cups water
  About 1 pound lean boneless beef (sirloin or top round)
1 **medium-size head garlic (about 20 cloves), finely chopped**
1 **large shallot or small onion, finely chopped**
1½ **teaspoons sugar**
1 **teaspoon turmeric**
1 **teaspoon shrimp paste or anchovy paste (optional)**
1 **tablespoon soy sauce**
4 **whole tamarind pods (each 4 to 5 inches long) or ½ cup tamarind pulp or lemon juice**
  Salt and crushed red pepper
  Fish sauce to taste

Cut lemon grass into 4-inch lengths, then tie pieces in a bundle (or tie sliced lemon grass in a piece of moistened cheesecloth or place in a tea ball). In a 3-quart pan, combine lemon grass, galangal, and 3 cups of the water. Bring to a boil over high heat; then cover, reduce heat to medium, and simmer for 10 minutes.

Cut beef into slices about ¼ inch thick and add to lemon grass mixture; then add garlic, shallot, sugar, turmeric, shrimp paste (if used), and soy. Cover and simmer until beef is tender when pierced (about 15 minutes). Discard shells and fibrous strands from tamarind pods; drop pulp into soup and simmer for 5 more minutes. Remove and discard lemon grass, galangal, and, if desired, tamarind seeds. Add more water if soup appears too thick. Season to taste with salt, pepper, and fish sauce. Makes 4 to 6 servings.

ข้าว Rice & Noodles

Festive Yellow Rice
(Pictured on facing page)

Once reserved for religious ceremonies, *nasi kuning* is still served on special occasions in Indonesia. This sweet and aromatic centerpiece of a dish is wonderful with satay (page 91).

 1 stalk fresh or dry lemon grass or 1 strip lemon peel (yellow part only), 1 inch wide and 4 to 5 inches long
 2½ cups long-grain rice
 1½ cups coconut milk (page 89)
 3 cups water
 2½ teaspoons turmeric
 1 teaspoon salt
 1 slice dry galangal (optional)
 1 bay leaf
 1 dry citrus leaf (optional)

Cut lemon grass into pieces and tie in a bundle as shown in photograph on facing page. In a 3-quart pan, combine lemon grass, rice, coconut milk, water, turmeric, salt, galangal (if used), bay leaf, and citrus leaf (if used). Bring to a boil over medium-high heat. Reduce heat to medium-low and simmer, uncovered, stirring gently every now and then, just until liquid is absorbed. To finish cooking, steam according to one of the methods described below. Makes 6 servings.

To steam in cooking pan: Cover pan, reduce heat to low, and cook until rice is tender (15 to 20 minutes). Halfway through estimated cooking time, gently fluff rice with 2 forks as shown in photograph on facing page. Remove and discard seasonings. Transfer to a serving bowl; or mound rice on a platter, a spoonful at a time, into a rounded cone.

To steam using the traditional method: Transfer rice and seasonings to a colander or steamer basket insert. Into a large kettle, pour water to a depth of 1½ inches; bring to a boil over high heat. Place colander in kettle. Cover, reduce heat, and steam until rice is tender (about 20 minutes). If made ahead, keep warm in steamer, covered, for up to 1 hour. Remove and discard seasonings; serve as directed above.

Spiced Rice

Throughout the Far East, rice is the heart of every meal. In *nasi minyak*, a Malaysian specialty, butter and sweet spices cook with the rice.

 4 cups long-grain rice
   Water
 ½ cup (¼ lb.) butter or margarine
 2 tablespoons minced shallot
 2 cloves garlic, minced or pressed
 1 tablespoon minced fresh ginger
 1 teaspoon ground coriander
 ½ teaspoon ground cumin
 2 or 3 whole star anise
 1 cinnamon stick (2 inches long)
 3 or 4 whole cloves
 3 whole cardamom pods, cracked open

Rinse rice with water until water runs clear; drain and set aside. In a 5 to 6-quart kettle over low heat, melt butter; add shallots, garlic, ginger, coriander, cumin, anise, cinnamon stick, cloves, and cardamom. Cook, stirring, for 4 to 5 minutes. Add rice and 7½ cups water. Increase heat to high and bring mixture to a boil; then cover, reduce heat, and cook until rice is tender to bite (about 20 minutes). Stir lightly with a fork; remove whole spices and use for garnish. Makes 8 to 10 servings.

Steamed Sticky Rice

In Laos and northern Thailand, sticky rice is the staple grain. It's traditionally steamed in a pot made especially for that purpose (see page 101).

 3 cups sticky rice (also called sweet or glutinous rice)
   Water

Soak rice in water to cover for at least 2 hours or until next day. Drain, rinse, and drain again. Place rice on a steaming rack lined with a clean towel. (If rack has no sides, loosely tie rice in towel.) Into a large pan, pour boiling water to a depth of 1½ inches; then place rack in pan. Cover and steam until rice is tender (about 20 minutes). Dump rice onto a dampened shallow tray or pan. With a wet spoon, lift and turn rice for 2 to 3 minutes to cool it slightly. Cover until ready to serve; serve warm or at room temperature. Makes about 4 servings.

Festive Yellow Rice

(Recipe on facing page) with Beef Satay (page 91), Spiced Coconut (page 96), Chili Paste (page 96), and Peanut Sauce (page 92)

1 Cut lemon grass in pieces; use outer layer of stalk to tie in a bundle. Dry galangal (left) and citrus leaf (center) also flavor rice.

2 Simmer rice just until liquid is absorbed. Then cover and steam in pan, or transfer to a steamer.

3 Halfway through steaming time, fluff rice in pan gently with two forks so it will cook evenly.

4 Mound cooked rice by spoonfuls on a platter to make a rounded cone; pat gently to neaten.

Soft-fried Noodles

Cooked rice noodles, stir-fried with pork, shrimp, and vegetables, make a savory entrée. A sweet-hot sauce melds all the flavors in this Thai supper dish.

Sweet-Hot Sauce (recipe follows)
Soy-Pepper Sauce (recipe follows)
12 cups water
6 ounces thin rice noodles (rice sticks)
5 tablespoons salad oil
¼ pound medium-size shrimp, shelled, deveined, and chopped
1 medium-size onion, chopped
½ pound ground pork
2 cloves garlic, minced or pressed
1 medium-size carrot, shredded
2 eggs, lightly beaten
¼ cup finely chopped roasted peanuts
Garnishes (see Crisp-fried Noodles, facing page)

Prepare Sweet-Hot Sauce and Soy-Pepper Sauce; set both aside. Pour water into a 4 to 5-quart kettle; bring to a boil over high heat. Add noodles and cook, uncovered, just until tender to bite (2 to 4 minutes). Drain, rinse with cold water, and drain again.

Heat 1 tablespoon of the oil in a wok or wide frying pan over high heat. Add shrimp and cook, stirring constantly, until pink (1 to 2 minutes); remove from pan and set aside. Add 1 more tablespoon oil; then add onion and crumble in pork. Cook, stirring, until pork is lightly browned (about 4 minutes). Add garlic and carrot and cook, stirring, for 1 more minute. Add 2 more tablespoons oil; add noodles and cook, stirring, until heated through.

Make a well in center of noodle mixture and pour in remaining 1 tablespoon oil. Pour eggs into well. Cook, stirring (keep eggs in well), just until eggs begin to set; then stir eggs into noodle mixture. Return shrimp to pan and add Sweet-Hot Sauce; stir to blend. Pour into a serving dish and sprinkle with peanuts. Surround with garnishes and serve with Soy-Pepper Sauce. Makes 3 or 4 servings.

Sweet-Hot Sauce. In a bowl, stir together 2 teaspoons *each* **white (distilled) vinegar** and **water**, ½ teaspoon **crushed red pepper**, 2 tablespoons **fish sauce** or soy sauce, and 1 tablespoon *each* minced **fresh coriander** (cilantro) and **sugar**.

Soy-Pepper Sauce. In a bowl, combine 6 tablespoons **soy sauce** and ½ to ¾ teaspoon **crushed red pepper**.

Pork & Shrimp Noodles

Like Chinese fried rice, Filipino *pansit* is a simple and thrifty meal that makes good use of small amounts of ingredients.

6 ounces thin rice noodles (rice sticks)
5 tablespoons salad oil
1 small onion, chopped
1 teaspoon minced fresh ginger
1 or 2 cloves garlic, minced or pressed
1½ cups *each* small cooked shrimp and diced cooked pork (such as roast or chops)
4 cups shredded, lightly packed bok choy
3 tablespoons oyster sauce
¼ cup regular-strength chicken broth
¼ teaspoon crushed red pepper
1 green onion (including top), minced

Soak noodles in warm water to cover for 20 minutes; drain. Heat 3 tablespoons of the oil in a wide frying pan over medium heat. Add noodles and cook, stirring, until heated through (about 1 minute). Transfer to a platter and keep warm.

Heat remaining 2 tablespoons oil in pan over high heat. Add onion, ginger, garlic, shrimp, and pork. Cook, stirring, for 1 minute. Stir in bok choy, oyster sauce, broth, and pepper. Cover; cook until bok choy wilts (about 1 minute). Spoon over noodles; top with green onion. Makes 3 or 4 servings.

Fresh Lumpia

The Chinese egg roll has its Filipino counterpart in *lumpia*: soft, light wrappers rolled around a filling of pork, shrimp, and bean sprouts.

About 18 Lumpia Wrappers, purchased or homemade (recipe follows)
Dipping Sauce (recipe follows)
Lumpia Filling (recipe follows)
About 18 small inner romaine lettuce leaves
½ cup chopped roasted peanuts (optional)
Small bunch fresh coriander (cilantro)
4 green onions (including tops), cut into thin lengthwise strips

Prepare Lumpia Wrappers, Dipping Sauce, and Lumpia Filling. For each lumpia, spread a wrapper with about 1 teaspoon of the sauce. Set a lettuce leaf on wrapper to extend from center over top edge. Spoon about 2 tablespoons of the filling on lettuce; top with some of the peanuts (if used), coriander, and onions. Fold lower half of wrapper over filling, then overlap sides to enclose. Eat out of hand. Serve with additional Dipping Sauce. Makes 6 to 8 servings.

Lumpia Wrappers. In a blender or food processor, combine 3 **eggs,** ¾ cup **cornstarch,** 1½ cups **cold water,** ½ teaspoon **salt,** and 1½ tablespoons **salad oil;** whirl until smooth. Also have ready a small dish of salad oil (you'll need about 1½ tablespoons *total*).

Heat a 6 to 7-inch crêpe pan (or other small frying pan) over medium heat until a drop of water sizzles when dropped on pan bottom. Remove pan from heat and grease with ¼ teaspoon of the oil. Using a ¼-cup measure, stir batter; then dip out 2 to 3 tablespoons. Pour, all at once, into pan. Quickly tilt pan to spread batter over bottom; return to heat and cook until wrapper looks dry on top (1½ to 2 minutes). Slide out of pan; let cool on paper towels. Repeat with remaining batter. Makes about 18.

Dipping Sauce. Combine 2 tablespoons **cornstarch** and ¼ cup firmly packed **brown sugar.** Mix in ½ cup *each* **cold water** and **pineapple juice,** ¼ cup **soy sauce,** and ¼ cup **palm vinegar** or 2 tablespoons *each* white (distilled) vinegar and water. Heat 1 teaspoon **salad oil** in a small pan over medium heat. Add 2 cloves **garlic,** minced or pressed, and cook just until lightly browned. Add juice mixture and cook, stirring, until sauce boils and thickens.

Lumpia Filling. Crumble ¾ pound **ground pork** into a wide frying pan over medium heat. Add 1 **onion,** chopped, and 3 cloves **garlic,** minced or pressed; cook, stirring, until onion is soft and meat is lightly browned (6 to 8 minutes). Add 6 ounces **medium-size shrimp,** shelled, deveined, and chopped, and 1 cup coarsely chopped **bean sprouts;** cook until shrimp turns pink (about 2 more minutes). Stir in 1½ tablespoons **soy sauce** and remove from heat. Before using, drain; add juices to Dipping Sauce, then stir ¼ cup sauce into filling.

Crisp-fried Noodles
(Pictured on page 87)

The Thai passion for noodles is evident in *mee krob,* a spectacular-looking dish of puffy, crunchy noodles in rich sauce. We've tampered with tradition a bit; our mee krob isn't nearly as sweet as the classic—almost candied—version served in Thailand.

⅓ cup **tamarind liquid** (directions follow) or **lemon juice**
   Salad oil
¼ pound **thin rice noodles** (rice sticks)
½ cup **sugar**
¼ cup **bean sauce** (also called yellow bean sauce)
2 tablespoons **tomato paste**
2 tablespoons **fish sauce** or **soy sauce**
1 small **onion,** finely chopped
4 cloves **garlic,** minced or pressed
½ pound lean boneless **pork** (butt or leg), trimmed of fat and cut into ⅛ by ½ by 2-inch strips
1 whole **chicken breast** (about 1 lb.), skinned, boned, and cut into strips as described for pork
½ pound medium-size **shrimp,** shelled and deveined
   Garnishes (suggestions follow)

Prepare tamarind liquid; set aside. Into a wok or wide, heavy pan, pour oil to a depth of 1 inch and heat to 375° on a deep-frying thermometer. Drop in about a sixth of the noodles. As they puff and expand, push them down into oil; then turn entire mass over when crackling stops. Cook until all are puffy and no longer crackling (about 15 seconds); remove and drain briefly on paper towels. Skim and discard any bits of noodles from oil before cooking next batch. Keep warm in a 200° oven.

In a bowl, stir together tamarind liquid, sugar, bean sauce, tomato paste, and fish sauce; set aside.

Heat 2 tablespoons oil in wok or wide frying pan over high heat. Add onion and garlic; stir-fry for 1 minute. Add pork and stir-fry for 3 more minutes. Add chicken and shrimp and stir-fry until shrimp turn pink (about 3 minutes). Stir in sauce mixture; cook, stirring, until sauce boils, thickens, and turns glossy (3 to 5 minutes). Remove from heat and let cool for 3 minutes. Using 2 forks, fold in noodles, about a fourth at a time, until all are lightly coated with sauce. Mound noodles on a platter; surround with garnishes. Serve immediately. Makes 4 servings.

Tamarind liquid. In a bowl, combine ⅓ cup **hot water** and 2½ tablespoons **packaged tamarind pulp** or a 4 to 5-inch-long whole tamarind pod (shell and coarse strings removed). Let stand for 30 minutes. Knead pulp from seeds; discard seeds.

Garnishes. Arrange around finished dish (or place on a separate serving plate): ⅓ pound **bean sprouts,** coarsely chopped; 3 **green onions** (including tops), cut into thin strips; and 1 **lime,** cut into wedges.

Fish Curry
(Recipe on facing page)

1 Puncture coconut eye with screwdriver; drain out coconut water; and serve as a beverage.

2 Aim hammer blows at midpoint of heat-induced crack to break coconut into pieces.

3 Pry carefully with a screwdriver to separate flesh from shell; whirl flesh with water in blender.

4 Purée of coconut flesh and water drains through cheesecloth; wring hard to extract every drop.

5 Coconut milk and spices make bright curry sauce. Tip pan occasionally to baste fish.

ข้าว Fish & Shellfish

Spiced Whole Fish

In *gulai ikan*, an Indonesian curry, tender fish is simmered in a fiery sauce silkened with coconut milk. (Adjust the heat to your liking by varying the number of chiles.) Hot cooked rice is a good foil for this spicy dish.

⅓ cup tamarind liquid (page 81) or lemon juice
1 whole mild-flavored, white-fleshed fish, such as rockfish, cleaned and scaled (2 to 3 lbs.); or 2 pounds fillets, *each* about 1 inch thick, cut into 3 by 5-inch pieces
1 medium-size onion, cut into chunks
3 to 5 small dried whole hot red chiles
1½ cups water
1 stalk fresh lemon grass or ¼ cup sliced dry lemon grass or yellow part of peel from 1 lemon
¾ teaspoon turmeric
1¼ teaspoons salt
1½ cups coconut milk (page 89)
Fresh mint leaves (optional)

Prepare tamarind liquid and set aside.

Remove and discard head and tail from fish. Wrap fish in moistened cheesecloth, folding edges together securely at top; set aside.

In a blender or food processor, combine onion, chiles, and ½ cup of the water. Whirl until smooth. Pour into a wide frying pan. Add remaining 1 cup water, lemon grass (place dry lemon grass in a tea ball), turmeric, and salt. Cover and simmer over medium heat for 15 minutes. Add tamarind liquid and simmer for 5 more minutes. Stir in coconut milk; then place wrapped fish in sauce. Cover and simmer gently over medium heat just until flesh inside looks opaque (about 20 minutes for whole fish, 10 minutes for fillets). To test, prod in thickest portion with a fork (choose a portion covered with only a single layer of cheesecloth). Transfer fish to a rimmed serving dish; remove cheesecloth. Simmer sauce, uncovered, stirring occasionally, for 5 minutes. Remove and discard lemon grass. Spoon sauce over fish; garnish with mint, if desired. Makes 4 servings.

Fish Curry
(Pictured on facing page)

A Malay native, transplanted to Seattle, gave us this recipe for her favorite fish curry. In the Northwest, her first choice of fish is salmon, but the sauce is also compatible with halibut. In preparing this dish, keep the heat low—the sauce should never even reach a simmer. This slow, gentle cooking produces exceptionally moist and succulent fish.

1 large coconut (2 to 2½ lbs.) or 4 cups packaged shredded unsweetened coconut
2 cups hot water
¼ cup ground coriander
1 tablespoon *each* ground cumin and minced fresh ginger
½ teaspoon *each* turmeric and ground red pepper (cayenne)
¼ cup water
¼ cup salad oil
1 teaspoon black or yellow mustard seeds
¼ cup finely chopped shallots
3 cloves garlic, minced or pressed
3½ to 4 pounds salmon or halibut steaks (*each* about 1¼ inches thick)
3 large tomatoes, quartered
Salt
Fresh coriander (cilantro) sprigs

Following the directions on page 89, prepare coconut milk from whole or shredded coconut, using the 2 cups hot water (see photos on facing page). You should have about 2 cups rich coconut milk. Set aside. In a small bowl, combine coriander, cumin, ginger, turmeric, and pepper; stir in the ¼ cup water to make a paste.

Heat oil in a 5 to 6-quart kettle over medium-high heat. Add mustard seeds and stir until seeds pop; then add shallots and garlic and cook, stirring, until soft. Add coriander mixture and cook, stirring, for 2 minutes. Stir in coconut milk; then carefully layer fish in kettle (fish need not be completely covered by liquid). Place tomatoes, skin side up, around edge of kettle. Heat just until liquid begins to quiver, then reduce heat to medium-low and cook, uncovered, just until fish looks opaque in center (about 30 minutes—to test, prod with a fork). Sauce should not have any active bubbles while cooking. Tip kettle occasionally during cooking to distribute heat evenly and to baste any exposed parts of fish. Transfer fish to a warm platter. Season sauce to taste with salt; spoon over fish. Garnish with coriander. Makes 6 to 8 servings.

Red Chili Crab

From Singapore comes this light but boldly seasoned dish of cracked crab in a gingery, peppery sauce. As you eat the crab, dunk the meat into the extra sauce.

¼ cup salad oil
10 cloves garlic, finely chopped
1-inch piece fresh ginger, finely chopped
1 cup regular-strength chicken broth
¼ cup tomato paste
¼ to ½ teaspoon crushed red pepper
1 teaspoon white wine vinegar
3 cleaned and cracked cooked whole Dungeness crabs (about 6 lbs. *total*)

In an 8 to 10-quart kettle, combine oil, garlic, and ginger. Cook over medium-high heat, stirring, until hot; then add broth, tomato paste, pepper, and vinegar. Bring to a boil.

Add crab; stir gently to blend thoroughly with sauce. Cover and cook just until crab is heated through. Transfer crab and sauce to a large platter. Makes about 6 servings.

Shrimp-topped Eggplant Slices

Creamy baked eggplant slices provide a mild-flavored base for a tangy, spicy-hot shrimp mixture. Cooling cucumber spears and hot cooked rice complement this Indonesian treat, called *sambel udang terong*.

3 tablespoons tamarind liquid (page 81) or lemon juice
1 large eggplant (about 1½ lbs.)
6 tablespoons salad oil
1 small onion, finely chopped
¾ pound medium-size shrimp, shelled, deveined, and finely chopped
2 tablespoons sugar
1 teaspoon *each* chili powder and salt
¼ to ½ teaspoon crushed red pepper
Hot cooked rice

Prepare tamarind liquid, using 3 tablespoons hot water and 1½ tablespoons pulp. Set aside.

Cut eggplant crosswise into ¾-inch-thick slices.

Brush both sides of slices with oil, using 4 tablespoons of the oil, and place in a shallow baking pan. Bake in a 450° oven for about 30 minutes or until browned and tender when pierced.

Heat remaining 2 tablespoons oil in a small frying pan over medium heat. Add onion and cook, stirring, until lightly browned. Add shrimp, sugar, chili powder, salt, pepper, and tamarind liquid. Cook, stirring, until shrimp turns pink and liquid has evaporated.

Arrange eggplant in a single layer on a platter; distribute hot shrimp mixture evenly over each slice. Serve with rice. Makes 2 or 3 servings.

Cool & Tangy Gingered Fish

Tart, sweet, and peppery hot flavors will make your palate tingle when you taste this main-dish salad from Thailand. Serve the salad as a warm-weather entrée, or spoon into lettuce cups and serve as an exotic appetizer.

Salad oil
1 pound skinned rockfish fillets
⅓ cup finely shredded fresh ginger
½ cup thin strips shallots or mild onion
½ cup lime juice
1½ tablespoons sugar
1 tablespoon fish sauce or soy sauce
½ cup minced roasted salted peanuts
Butter or green leaf lettuce leaves
Fresh coriander (cilantro) sprigs

Pour enough oil into a wide frying pan to coat bottom; place over medium-high heat. Add fish and cook until lightly browned outside and opaque inside (about 10 minutes for a 1-inch-thick piece; cut a slash to test). Let cool; then finely shred with your hands. Mix fish with ginger and shallots.

In a small bowl, stir together lime juice, sugar, and fish sauce until sugar is dissolved. Mix with fish. (At this point, you may cover and refrigerate for up to 4 hours.)

Just before serving, stir in peanuts. Place fish mixture on a serving plate. Arrange lettuce leaves around edge of plate; garnish fish with coriander. Or, to serve fish mixture as an appetizer, spoon into lettuce leaves and top with coriander; then roll up and eat out of hand. Makes 10 to 12 appetizer servings or 4 main-dish servings.

ข้าว Poultry

Chicken & Pork Adobo

Probably the best-known dish from the Philippines is *adobo*, a hearty stew containing one or several types of meat simmered in soy and vinegar.

    1¼ pounds lean boneless pork (butt or leg)
    1   slice (about ⅓ lb.) baby beef liver (optional)
    4   *each* chicken legs and thighs
    1   cup palm vinegar or ½ cup *each* white
        (distilled) vinegar and water
    ¼   cup soy sauce
    ¼   teaspoon pepper
    1   bay leaf
    4   cloves garlic, minced or pressed
    2   tablespoons salad oil
        Chopped parsley
        Hot cooked rice

Discard fat from pork; cut meat into 1-inch cubes. Place in a bowl; add liver (if used) and chicken. Pour in vinegar and soy; add pepper, bay leaf, and garlic. Cover and refrigerate for 1 hour, turning occasionally.

Remove meat from marinade and pat dry; reserve marinade. Heat oil in a 5 to 6-quart kettle over medium-high heat. Add liver (if used) and cook just until firm (about 3 minutes); lift out and set aside. Add chicken and cook until browned on both sides; remove and set aside. Add pork and cook, stirring, until browned on all sides. Pour in marinade; cover, reduce heat to medium-low, and simmer for 15 minutes. Return chicken to kettle; cover and simmer until meat near thighbone is no longer pink when slashed and pork is tender when pierced (about 30 minutes). Dice liver (if used), return to kettle, and cook for about 2 minutes. Transfer all meat to a platter; cover and keep warm. Skim and discard fat from cooking liquid; remove and discard bay leaf. Boil liquid over high heat until reduced to about 1 cup; pour over meat. Sprinkle with parsley and serve over rice. Makes about 6 servings.

Pork Adobo

Follow directions for **Chicken & Pork Adobo,** but omit chicken and use about 2½ pounds **lean boneless pork.** Simmer for about 45 minutes.

Chicken Adobo

Follow directions for **Chicken & Pork Adobo,** but omit pork and use 6 *each* **chicken legs and thighs.** Simmer for about 30 minutes.

Barbecued Chicken in Soy Sauce

Satay without skewers best describes *ayam panggang*: crisp-skinned chicken flavored with a slightly sweet and tart soy marinade. A simple foil for any of the highly spiced dishes that Indonesia is renowned for, it's delightful with Festive Yellow Rice (page 78) and Spiced Coconut (page 96).

    1   small onion, quartered
    1   clove garlic, halved
    2   tablespoons water
    2   tablespoons salad oil
    ½   teaspoon Chili Paste (page 96) or crushed red
        pepper
    6   tablespoons soy sauce
    2   tablespoons *each* lemon juice and sugar
    ¼   teaspoon pepper
    1   frying chicken (3 to 3½ lbs.), cut into pieces

Place onion, garlic, and water in a blender or food processor; whirl until well minced.

Heat oil in a 10-inch frying pan over medium-high heat; add onion mixture and Chili Paste and cook, stirring often, until liquid has evaporated and mixture is lightly browned (about 10 minutes). Remove from heat and stir in soy, lemon juice, sugar, and pepper; let cool. Place chicken in a bowl; pour in soy mixture and turn chicken to coat all pieces. Cover and refrigerate for at least 4 hours or until next day.

To barbecue: Lift chicken from marinade, drain briefly, and arrange on a lightly greased grill 4 to 6 inches above a solid bed of medium-glowing coals. Cook, uncovered, turning frequently and basting occasionally with marinade, until meat near thighbone is no longer pink when slashed (45 to 55 minutes).

To roast: Lift chicken from marinade, drain briefly, and arrange skin side down on a lightly greased rack in a broiler pan. Bake in a 375° oven, uncovered, basting occasionally with marinade and turning once, for 45 to 55 minutes or until meat near thighbone is no longer pink when slashed. Makes 4 servings.

Fried Chicken Filipino

Chicken is a popular choice for family dinners the world over. In this Filipino favorite, chicken is served on a bed of mellow-sweet onions.

    4 tablespoons butter or margarine
    2 medium-size onions, thinly sliced
    ¼ cup all-purpose flour
    ½ teaspoon paprika
    4 *each* chicken legs and thighs
      About 2 tablespoons salad oil
    2 hard-cooked eggs
    ¼ cup minced fresh coriander (cilantro)
      Salt and pepper

In a wide frying pan over medium heat, melt 2 tablespoons of the butter. Add onions and cook, stirring, until very soft and lightly browned (about 20 minutes). Transfer to a serving dish; keep warm.

In a plastic bag, combine flour and paprika. Place chicken, a few pieces at a time, in bag; shake to coat. Remove from bag and shake off excess flour mixture. In pan over medium heat, melt remaining 2 tablespoons butter in 2 tablespoons of the oil; heat until surface of oil mixture ripples when pan is tilted. Add chicken and cook, turning frequently, until skin is crisp and browned (about 35 minutes), adding more oil as necessary. As chicken finishes cooking, remove and drain briefly on paper towels. Place in serving dish; stir to mix with onions.

Chop eggs; place in a bowl and stir in coriander. Season to taste with salt and pepper; sprinkle over chicken. Makes 4 servings.

Singapore Satay
(Pictured on front cover)

In Singapore, *satay* is flavored in a curry-spiked marinade and dipped in peanut sauce made spicy with chiles and garlic.

    2 tablespoons *each* curry powder and sugar
    ½ cup *each* salad oil and soy sauce
    4 cloves garlic, minced or pressed
    3 to 4 pounds skinned and boned chicken (breast or thigh)
      Peanut Sauce (page 92)
      Pressed Rice Cubes (recipe follows)

In a small bowl, stir together curry powder, sugar, oil, soy, and garlic. Cut chicken into ¾-inch cubes and place in a plastic bag. Pour in marinade; seal bag. Refrigerate, turning occasionally, for 2 hours.

Meanwhile, prepare Peanut Sauce and Pressed Rice Cubes; set aside.

Thread chicken on bamboo skewers; cook as directed for beef in Beef or Pork Satay (page 91). Serve chicken and rice cubes with Peanut Sauce. Makes 6 to 8 servings.

Pressed Rice Cubes. In a 2-quart pan, combine 1½ cups **short-grain (pearl) rice** and 2½ cups **water.** Bring to a boil over medium-high heat; then cover, reduce heat, and simmer just until water is absorbed (about 25 minutes). Pour hot rice into a 9-inch square pan. Using the back of a metal spoon or a wide spatula (rinse with water to prevent sticking), press rice down firmly to form an even layer. Let cool.

Run a knife around edge of pan and turn rice out onto a cutting board. Cut into 1-inch cubes, rinsing knife frequently. Arrange on a platter and serve at room temperature. Makes 6 to 8 servings.

Chicken with Mint

Goi ga & banh phong tom is a sprightly Vietnamese salad, lively with lime and mint.

    1 medium-size onion, thinly sliced
    3 tablespoons *each* sugar and white (distilled) vinegar
    ¼ teaspoon pepper
    2 tablespoons lime juice
    2 tablespoons fish sauce or soy sauce
    1 clove garlic, minced or pressed
    ¼ cup salad oil
    4 cups finely shredded cabbage
    2 cups *each* shredded carrots and shredded cooked chicken
    ⅓ cup shredded fresh mint
      About 36 small shrimp chips, fried as directed on page 95

In a bowl, mix together onion, sugar, vinegar, and pepper. Cover and refrigerate for at least 30 minutes or until next day.

Stir lime juice, fish sauce, garlic, and oil into marinated onion; then stir in cabbage, carrots, and chicken. Spoon into a serving dish and sprinkle with mint; offer shrimp chips as an accompaniment. Makes 4 to 6 servings.

Crisp-fried Noodles *(Recipe on page 81)*

1 Combine hot water with pulp from tamarind pods (left) or packaged pulp to make tart and fruity liquid.

2 Small tangle of wiry rice sticks hits hot oil. Almost immediately, noodles puff to an opaque white mass.

3 When crackling sound stops, use two spatulas to lift and turn large mound of cooked noodles.

4 Work quickly to fold noodles into sauce: serve immediately; sauce will soften noodles' crunch.

Chicken Curry with Condiments

At the heart of a good Burmese curry is a mixture of slowly cooked onions and turmeric that adds flavor and body to the finished sauce.

¾ cup **salad oil**
¼ teaspoon **turmeric**
3 large **onions,** chopped
4 cloves **garlic,** minced or pressed
2 tablespoons finely chopped **fresh ginger**
1 teaspoon **ground red pepper (cayenne)**
2 tablespoons **curry powder**
½ teaspoon **ground cumin**
6 whole **chicken breasts** (about 6 lbs. *total*), skinned, boned, and cut into 1-inch chunks
1 **bay leaf**
1 **cinnamon stick** (2½ to 3 inches long)
8 cups **regular-strength chicken broth**
1½ cups **coconut milk** (facing page)
Chinese Noodles (double recipe; page 28)
¾ cup **yellow split pea powder** or ½ cup **cornstarch**
1 cup **water**
Fish sauce or **soy sauce**
Condiments (suggestions follow)
Fried chiles (directions follow)

Heat ½ cup of the oil in a 5 to 6-quart kettle over low heat. Stir in turmeric and cook for about 1 minute. Add onions and cook, stirring occasionally, until very soft but not browned (about 20 minutes). Add garlic, ginger, pepper, curry powder, and cumin; cook, stirring, for about 1 minute. Add chicken, bay leaf, and cinnamon stick; stir to coat chicken evenly with spice mixture. Add broth; cover and bring to a boil over high heat. Add coconut milk. Cover, reduce heat to medium, and simmer until chicken is no longer pink when slashed (about 10 minutes). Meanwhile, prepare a double recipe of Chinese Noodles. Mix cooked noodles with remaining ¼ cup oil; let cool to room temperature.

In a bowl, combine split pea powder and water. Stir into curry. Reduce heat to low; cook, stirring, until sauce is slightly thickened (about 5 minutes). Season to taste with fish sauce.

Let each diner place some of the noodles in a bowl, top with hot curry, and add condiments and fried chiles. Makes 10 to 12 servings.

Condiments. In separate bowls, place about ½ cup chopped **fresh coriander** (cilantro), ½ cup thinly sliced **green onions** (including tops), 6 **hard-cooked eggs,** thinly sliced, 2 to 3 cups **crisp-fried chow mein noodles,** and 2 **lemons,** cut into wedges.

Fried chiles. Place 1½ tablespoons **crushed red pepper** and 2 teaspoons **salad oil** in a small pan over low heat; cook, stirring, just until pepper begins to brown (about 2 minutes). Serve at room temperature.

Thai Red Curry

Our Thai chicken curry is flavored with a freshly made red curry paste that cooks in the oil from coconut milk.

2 cups **fresh coconut milk** (facing page)
Red Curry Paste (recipe follows)
4 *each* **chicken legs** and **thighs,** skinned
Fish sauce, soy sauce, or **salt**

Prepare coconut milk from whole or packaged shredded coconut. Cover and refrigerate for at least 2 hours or until next day; milk will separate into a top layer of thick cream and a bottom layer of thin milk. Skim off all cream; place in a measuring cup and add thin milk, if necessary, to make 1 cup total. Set aside remaining thin coconut milk.

Prepare Red Curry Paste; set aside. Place coconut cream in a heavy 4 to 5-quart kettle; bring to a boil over medium-high heat, stirring constantly. Reduce heat to medium and continue cooking until cream looks shiny on top and is reduced to about ¼ cup (about 10 minutes). Add curry paste and cook, stirring, until mixture thickens slightly and again looks shiny on top (about 5 minutes). Add chicken and turn to coat evenly with curry mixture. Stir in remaining thin coconut milk (about 1 cup). Cover, reduce heat, and simmer, stirring occasionally, until meat near thighbone is no longer pink when slashed (40 to 45 minutes). Add fish sauce to taste. If made ahead, let cool; then cover and refrigerate until next day. Reheat over medium heat, stirring occasionally, until heated through. Makes 4 servings.

Red Curry Paste. In a blender or food processor, combine 2 teaspoons **ground coriander;** 2 teaspoons sliced **fresh lemon grass** or grated lemon peel; 1 or 2 **small dried whole hot red chiles,** stemmed and seeded; ½ teaspoon **shrimp paste** or anchovy paste (optional); 1 teaspoon *each* **ground cumin, paprika,** and chopped **fresh ginger;** 4 cloves **garlic,** halved; and 1 small **onion,** cut into chunks. Whirl until smooth.

The Coconut

Legend has it that the coconut was named by traders from Spain and Portugal, who apparently thought that the shell's three "eyes" resembled the face of a clown: loosely translated, the Spanish word *coco* means "grinning face."

The coconut is native to the tropics, where it's used in hundreds of different ways. Coconut water—the liquid you hear sloshing inside a fresh nut—is drunk fresh, or fermented into a potent alcoholic beverage. The flesh of the nut is eaten as is, of course, but it's also used to produce coconut milk, a staple ingredient in Southeast Asian cooking. Coconuts also yield a high grade of vegetable oil, used both for cooking and in the manufacture of soaps, candles, and cosmetics. This oil can be produced a bit at a time (the Thai way—see facing page) or in quantity.

The fruit requires about a year to ripen into the hard, brown, fibrous-shelled form most familiar to us. But immature coconuts are edible, too—in the tropics, they're enjoyed for their soft, jellylike texture. Fresh green coconuts aren't available outside the tropics, but you can buy them preserved in jars in Oriental (especially Filipino) markets. They're labeled "macapuno strings" or "macapuno balls."

Fresh, fully ripened coconut makes the most flavorful coconut milk. To check for freshness, first look to be sure all three eyes are closed; then shake the coconut. You should hear liquid sloshing inside: the more liquid, the fresher the coconut.

Fresh Coconut Milk

> 1 fresh coconut
> Hot water

To prepare coconut milk (see photos, page 82), first pierce eyes with a screwdriver or an ice pick. Pour out the liquid inside; reserve and serve as a beverage, if desired. Place drained coconut on a rimmed baking sheet in a 350° oven for about 15 minutes or just until shell begins to crack. Let cool briefly, then place on a sturdy surface. Using a hammer or mallet, hit hard along the crack; the nut should break into pieces.

Pry white flesh from shell with a screwdriver or knife with a rounded end. If desired, pare off brown skin with a small knife or vegetable peeler. Break flesh into small chunks; then transfer to a blender or food processor and whirl until coarsely chopped. Measure coconut and return to blender with an equal amount of very hot water. Whirl again (in batches, if necessary) until mixture is a thick, pulpy mass. Pour into a sieve lined with moistened cheesecloth; let drain briefly into a deep bowl, then gather cheesecloth and squeeze firmly to extract all remaining liquid. One cup *each* coconut and water makes about 1 cup coconut milk. (This first extraction is called thick coconut milk. You can repeat the process once or twice, but milk will be thinner and weaker each time. All recipes in this book were tested with thick coconut milk.) Discard coconut flesh; cover milk and refrigerate for up to 3 days, or freeze for longer storage. Milk which has been stored will separate into a top layer of thick cream and a bottom layer of thin milk; stir to reblend before using in recipes calling for coconut milk.

Coconut Cream

Pour **Fresh Coconut Milk** into a glass bowl or measuring cup. Cover and refrigerate for at least 2 hours or until next day. The thick white liquid that rises to the top is called coconut cream; it's an ingredient in some sauces and desserts—Sticky Rice with Mangoes, for example (page 97). What settles below the cream is thin coconut milk. If a recipe calls for coconut milk, stir to reblend cream with milk.

Coconut Milk in a Hurry

Follow directions for **Fresh Coconut Milk,** but substitute packaged **shredded unsweetened coconut** for fresh coconut.

Alternatives to fresh. Prepared coconut milk is available canned or frozen in Oriental markets and in some well-stocked supermarkets. (Many brands are imported from Hawaii, Thailand, and the Philippines.) Check the label to make sure that the coconut milk you buy is unsweetened. Most brands of canned coconut milk are as thick as homemade coconut cream; dilute with water, if desired.

You can make a convenient (though not authentic) substitute for fresh or canned coconut milk by mixing whipping cream with coconut extract (sold alongside vanilla in the supermarket). Use ½ teaspoon *each* **sugar** and **coconut extract** and 1 cup **whipping cream** for every cup of coconut milk. This coconut-flavored cream won't separate into thick cream and thin milk, so don't use it in recipes such as Thai Red Curry (facing page) in which the cream from fresh coconut is an essential ingredient.

ข้าว Meats

Laotian Steak Tartare

Laub could be called the national dish of Laos. It's based on finely minced raw beef, seasoned with lots of fresh herbs. Sticky rice (preferred over short or long-grain rice in Laos) and assorted fresh vegetables are served alongside.

Steamed Sticky Rice (page 78)
- 3 tablespoons raw sticky rice (also called glutinous or sweet rice)
- 2 slices dry galangal or 2 thin slices fresh ginger
- 1 pound lean boneless beef (sirloin or top round)
- 2 tablespoons anchovy cream or anchovy paste, mixed with 3 tablespoons boiling water and allowed to cool (optional)
- 1 to 2 teaspoons fish sauce or soy sauce
- 3 tablespoons lime juice
- ½ to 1 teaspoon ground red pepper (cayenne)
- ½ cup *each* sliced fresh lemon grass, chopped fresh coriander (cilantro), and sliced green onions (including tops)
- 1 large cucumber, thinly sliced
  Butter or leaf lettuce leaves
- 1 bunch radishes
  Thin cabbage wedges

Prepare Steamed Sticky Rice; set aside.

In a small frying pan over low heat, toast the 3 tablespoons rice, stirring frequently, until golden (about 5 minutes); whirl in a blender or food processor until finely ground and set aside.

Pound galangal with a mortar and pestle until finely crushed (or finely chop ginger); set aside.

Trim and discard excess fat from beef. Cut meat into very thin shreds (or cut into chunks, then whirl in a food processor until coarsely ground).

In a large bowl, combine beef, ground rice, anchovy cream mixture (if used), galangal, fish sauce, lime juice, pepper, lemon grass, coriander, and onions. Place on a platter. Serve at room temperature, accompanied with cucumber, lettuce, radishes, cabbage, and Steamed Sticky Rice. To eat, roll a small amount of rice into a ball with your hands; use rice to scoop up some of the meat mixture. Accompany with vegetables. Makes about 4 servings.

Simmered Beef in Rice Paper

"Fun to eat" describes this cook-at-the-table meal from Vietnam. You fold moistened rice paper around fillings—tender noodles, fresh vegetables, and beef—and eat the packet out of hand.

Dipping Sauce (recipe follows)
- 8 cups water
- 4 ounces thin rice noodles (rice sticks)
- 1½ to 2 pounds lean boneless beef (sirloin or top round)
- 1 large cucumber
- ½ pound bean sprouts
- 2 large heads butter lettuce, separated into leaves
- 1 bunch fresh coriander (cilantro)
  Lemony Broth (recipe follows)
- 10 large rice paper rounds, each about 12 inches in diameter (optional)

Prepare Dipping Sauce; set aside.

Pour water into a large kettle; bring to a boil over high heat. Add noodles and cook just until tender to bite (3 to 4 minutes). Drain, rinse with cold water, and drain again.

Trim and discard excess fat from meat; then slice into thin 4-inch-long strips. Arrange on a platter.

Peel or score cucumber, if desired. Cut in half lengthwise, then cut each half crosswise into thin slices. Arrange cucumber, bean sprouts, lettuce, and coriander in bowls or on platters. (At this point, you may cover and refrigerate noodles, meat, and vegetables separately for up to 6 hours.)

Shortly before serving, prepare Lemony Broth. Pour steaming broth into a fondue pot or chafing dish; place over heat source at the table.

Cut each rice paper round into thirds; place on the table with a water mister or spray bottle alongside.

Set platters of prepared meat and vegetables on the table. Provide each diner with a bowl of Dipping Sauce. Place a few strips of beef in bubbling broth; while meat cooks, mist rice paper with water. When paper is pliable, line with a lettuce leaf and top with noodles, a strip of beef, and vegetables. (Or omit rice paper and use lettuce leaf alone as wrapper.) Wrap sides around to form a small packet; dip into sauce and eat out of hand. Makes 4 to 6 servings.

Dipping Sauce. In a bowl, stir together ¾ cup **fish sauce** or soy sauce, ½ cup **cider vinegar**, ⅔ cup **sugar**, 3 tablespoons **water**, ½ to 1 teaspoon **crushed**

red pepper, and 2 cloves **garlic,** minced or pressed. Add ¾ cup finely shredded **carrot;** stir well. Divide sauce among 4 to 6 small bowls.

Lemony Broth. In a pan, combine 4 cups **water,** ½ cup **cider vinegar,** ⅓ cup **sugar,** 3 quarter-size slices **fresh ginger,** and 3 **chicken bouillon cubes.** Then add 1 stalk **fresh or dry lemon grass** (cut into 4-inch lengths and tied in a bundle) or ¼ cup sliced dry lemon grass (tied in moistened cheesecloth or placed in a tea ball) or yellow part of peel from 1 lemon. Simmer over medium heat, covered, until hot (about 10 minutes).

Dry Beef Curry

In Sumatra's tropical climate, spices are valued for their ability to preserve food. Of course, they're also prized for their taste; in Indonesian *rendang,* a rich, sweet, and spicy coconut-milk sauce imparts a delicious flavor to chunks of beef.

   ½ **cup tamarind liquid (page 81)**
   2 **tablespoons salad oil**
   2 **pounds lean boneless beef (chuck), cut into 1½-inch chunks**
   1 **medium-size onion, chopped**
   4 **cloves garlic, minced or pressed**
   1 **tablespoon** *each* **chopped fresh ginger and ground coriander**
   1 **cinnamon stick (2½ to 3 inches long)**
   1 **teaspoon ground cumin**
   1 **teaspoon Chili Paste (page 96) or crushed red pepper**
   ½ **teaspoon** *each* **pepper and ground cloves**
   ½ **teaspoon shrimp paste or anchovy paste (optional)**
 2½ **cups coconut milk (page 89)**
      Hot cooked rice

Prepare tamarind liquid, using ½ cup hot water and ¼ cup pulp. Set aside.

Heat oil in a wok or 5-quart kettle over medium-high heat; add meat, a few pieces at a time, and cook until browned on all sides. Lift out and set aside. Add onion, garlic, and ginger; cook, stirring, until onion is soft. Add coriander, cinnamon stick, cumin, Chili Paste, pepper, cloves, and shrimp paste (if used). Cook, stirring, until seasonings are well combined. Return beef to kettle; stir to coat with spice mixture. Stir in tamarind liquid and coconut milk. Bring to a boil; then cover, reduce heat to medium-low, and simmer, stirring occasionally, un-

til meat is very tender when pierced and sauce is very thick and almost dry (1½ to 2 hours). Remove and discard cinnamon stick; spoon off and discard fat from sauce. Serve with rice. Makes 6 to 8 servings.

Beef Chiang Mai

In northern Thailand lies "the city of roses"—Chiang Mai, where flowers, especially roses, bloom profusely in the temperate mountain climate. Warm, spicy beef wrapped in cool lettuce leaves is a traditional dish of the region, equally good as a light supper entrée or an appetizer.

   ¼ **cup short-grain (pearl) or long-grain rice**
   1 **pound lean ground beef**
   1 **teaspoon** *each* **sugar and crushed red pepper**
   ½ **cup** *each* **thinly sliced green onions (including tops) and chopped fresh mint**
   2 **tablespoons chopped fresh coriander (cilantro)**
   ¼ **cup lemon juice**
 1½ **tablespoons soy sauce**
      Small inner leaves from 2 large or 3 small heads butter lettuce
      About 36 fresh mint sprigs

In a wok or wide frying pan over medium heat, toast rice, shaking pan frequently, until golden (5 to 8 minutes). Remove from heat and transfer to a blender or food processor; whirl until finely ground.

Crumble beef into pan; cook over low heat, stirring, just until meat begins to lose its pinkness. Add ground rice, sugar, pepper, onions, the chopped mint, coriander, lemon juice, and soy; stir until well combined. Pour into a serving dish and surround with lettuce leaves and mint sprigs. Spoon beef mixture into lettuce, top with a mint sprig, roll up, and eat out of hand. Makes about 12 appetizer servings or 3 or 4 main-dish servings.

Beef or Pork Satay
(Pictured on page 79)

Perhaps no Southeast Asian food is better known than *satay:* Indonesia, Malaysia, and Singapore all claim it as their national dish. In this Indonesian version, cubes of beef or pork are grilled and served with a spicy-hot peanut sauce.

(Continued on next page)

1½ pounds lean boneless beef (sirloin or top round) or pork (butt or leg)
1 clove garlic, minced or pressed
2 tablespoons soy sauce
1 tablespoon salad oil
1 teaspoon *each* ground cumin and coriander
   Basting Sauce (recipe follows)
   Peanut Sauce (recipe follows)
   Chili Paste (page 96)

Cut meat into ¾-inch cubes. In a bowl, stir together garlic, soy, oil, cumin, and coriander. Add meat and stir to coat evenly. Cover and refrigerate for 1½ to 2 hours. Meanwhile, prepare Basting Sauce, Peanut Sauce, and Chili Paste; set aside.

Thread about 4 cubes of meat on each of about 18 small bamboo skewers. Place on a lightly greased grill 4 to 6 inches above a solid bed of medium-glowing coals (or place on a rack in a broiler pan about 4 to 6 inches below heat); cook, turning often, until beef is done to your liking when slashed (8 to 10 minutes for medium-rare) or until pork is no longer pink when slashed (about 15 minutes). Three minutes before end of estimated cooking time, brush meat all over with Basting Sauce. Serve with Peanut Sauce and Chili Paste. Makes 4 to 6 servings.

Basting Sauce. In a small bowl, stir together 3 tablespoons **lemon juice**, 2 tablespoons **soy sauce**, and ¼ teaspoon *each* **ground cumin** and **coriander**.

Peanut Sauce. In a small pan, combine 1 cup **water**, ⅔ cup creamy or crunchy **peanut butter**, and 2 cloves **garlic**, minced or pressed. Cook over medium heat, stirring, until mixture boils and thickens. Remove from heat and stir in 2 tablespoons **brown sugar**, 1½ tablespoons **lemon juice**, 1 tablespoon **soy sauce**, and ¼ to ½ teaspoon **Chili Paste** (page 96) or crushed red pepper. Let cool to room temperature before serving. If made ahead, cover and refrigerate until next day; to reheat, cook over medium-low heat, stirring, until hot. Thin with water, if necessary, to make a medium-thick sauce. Makes about 2 cups.

Skewered Pork & Onion

Here's a Vietnamese treat for the barbecue: squares of lemony pork wrapped around juicy onion chunks, then skewered and grilled.

2 pounds lean boneless pork (butt or leg)
   Lemon Grass Marinade (recipe follows)
   Dipping Sauce (recipe follows)
1 large onion, cut into 1-inch squares

Have meatman cut pork into 3/16-inch-thick slices; cut slices into 2-inch squares. Prepare Lemon Grass Marinade. Mix meat with marinade; cover and refrigerate for at least 2 hours. Prepare Dipping Sauce.

Separate onion squares into 2-layer pieces. Place an onion piece on each meat square, wrap meat around onion, and thread on a bamboo skewer. (Place 4 to 6 meat-onion pieces on each skewer.)

Place on a grill 2 inches above a solid bed of glowing coals; cook, turning occasionally, until meat is no longer pink when slashed (10 to 15 minutes). Serve with Dipping Sauce. Makes 8 servings.

Lemon Grass Marinade. In a food processor or blender, whirl until smooth: 2 tablespoons chopped **fresh or dry lemon grass** (if dry, soak in warm water for 30 minutes before using), 1 **onion**, quartered, 3 cloves **garlic**, 3 tablespoons **sugar**, 2 tablespoons **roasted peanuts**, 1 tablespoon **fish sauce** or soy sauce, 1½ teaspoons **pepper**, and 1 teaspoon **Chinese five-spice** (or ¼ teaspoon *each* crushed anise seeds and ground cinnamon, cloves, and ginger).

Dipping Sauce. In a bowl, stir together 2 tablespoons **fish sauce** or soy sauce, 1 tablespoon **lime juice**, 2 cloves **garlic**, minced or pressed, 2 tablespoons **sugar**, ¼ cup **warm water**, and 2 tablespoons finely shredded **carrot**. Stir until sugar is dissolved.

Ribs Filipino

Ribs are a universal favorite, a top choice for casual dining. Our version from the Philippines is spicy with star anise and ginger.

3 medium-size onions
5 to 6 pounds pork spareribs, cut into individual ribs
6 tablespoons soy sauce
¼ teaspoon pepper
6 whole star anise
1 tablespoon salad oil
1 tablespoon grated or minced fresh ginger
½ cup honey
2 tablespoons brown sugar
1 tablespoon *each* Worcestershire and lemon juice

Cut 2 of the onions into wedges; place in a 5 to 6-quart kettle along with ribs, 4 tablespoons of the soy, pepper, and anise. Bring to a boil over high heat; then cover, reduce heat to medium-low, and simmer in juices that cook out of meat, stirring occasionally, until ribs are tender when pierced (1 to 1¼ hours).

Meanwhile, finely chop remaining onion. Heat oil in a wide frying pan over medium heat and add onion. Cook, stirring, until soft. Add ginger, honey, sugar, Worcestershire, lemon juice, and remaining 2 tablespoons soy. Cook, stirring, until well mixed. Remove from heat.

With tongs, lift ribs from kettle and arrange in a single layer in a shallow roasting pan or broiler pan (about 11 by 16 inches). Brush honey mixture evenly over ribs. Bake, uncovered, in a 400° oven, basting often with pan drippings, for about 30 minutes or until ribs are well glazed. Makes 4 to 6 servings.

Simmered Pork

In the Philippines, *tocino* is often spooned over cooked rice, then wrapped and transported in banana leaves (see page 104) for a picnic dish.

>   2 to 2½ pounds lean boneless pork (butt or leg)
>   2 cloves garlic, minced or pressed
>   ½ cup palm vinegar or ¼ cup *each* white (distilled) vinegar and water
>   ½ cup soy sauce
>   ½ teaspoon pepper
>   ½ teaspoon saltpeter (optional)
>   ¼ cup sugar
>   About 1 tablespoon salad oil

Cut pork into slices about ¼ inch thick and 3 inches long. In a bowl, mix garlic, vinegar, soy, pepper, saltpeter (if used), and sugar; stir until sugar is dissolved. Add pork; cover and refrigerate for at least 8 hours or until next day, stirring occasionally. Heat 1 tablespoon of the oil in a wide frying pan (preferably one with a nonstick finish) over medium heat. Remove about a third of the pork from marinade, drain briefly, and arrange in a single layer in pan. Cook, turning occasionally, until liquid has evaporated. Reduce heat to medium-low; continue cooking until meat is browned on all sides. Remove to a serving plate, cover, and, if desired, keep warm in a 200° oven. Repeat with remaining pork, adding more oil to pan as necessary. Serve warm or at room temperature. Makes about 6 servings.

Coffee & Tea the Thai Way

In Thailand, strongly brewed coffee and tea are lightly spiced, then smoothed with a spoonful or two of sweetened condensed or evaporated milk. The result is a rich-tasting beverage that can be served hot or cold—it's almost like a dessert.

Cardamom-spiced Coffee

>   ¾ cup ground coffee
>   2⅔ cups water
>   Ground cardamom
>   About ½ cup sweetened condensed milk

Using amounts specified above, brew coffee in a drip-style coffee maker or percolator. Pour into 4 cups. To each serving, add a dash of ground cardamom and about 2 tablespoons of the condensed milk; stir to blend. Makes 4 servings.

Thai Iced Coffee

Brew coffee as directed for **Cardamom-spiced Coffee;** let cool slightly. Fill four 10 to 12-ounce beverage glasses to the rim with **ice cubes;** then fill two-thirds full with coffee. Into each glass, stir about 2 tablespoons **evaporated milk** (you'll need about ½ cup *total*); add a dash of **ground cardamom** and sweeten to taste with **sugar.** Makes 4 servings.

Cinnamon-spiced Tea

>   8 Chinese-style red or black tea bags or ¼ cup regular black tea
>   4 cups boiling water
>   Ground cinnamon
>   About ½ cup sweetened condensed milk

Place tea in a teapot; pour water over tea. Let steep for 5 minutes. Pour into 4 cups. To each serving, add a dash of cinnamon and about 2 tablespoons of the condensed milk; stir to blend. Makes 4 servings.

Thai Iced Tea

Brew tea as directed for **Cinnamon-spiced Tea;** let cool slightly. Fill four 10 to 12-ounce beverage glasses to the rim with **ice cubes;** then fill two-thirds full with tea. Into each glass, stir about 2 tablespoons **evaporated milk** (you'll need about ½ cup *total*); add a dash of **ground cinnamon** and sweeten to taste with **sugar.** Makes 4 servings.

ข้าว Vegetables & Condiments

Wilted Romaine with Hot Sausage Dressing

This Thai combination of crisp, cool greens and warm, peppery-sweet dressing makes an unusual first course or a refreshing warm-weather entrée.

> Lime Dressing (recipe follows)
> 12 cups bite-size pieces romaine lettuce (about 1 large head)
> 1 small cucumber, thinly sliced
> 1 large tomato, cut into wedges
> 1 small red onion, thinly sliced
> ½ cup fresh coriander (cilantro) leaves
> About ⅓ pound (4 or 5) Chinese sausages (*lop cheong*) or dry salami
> 2 tablespoons salad oil
> 4 cloves garlic, minced or pressed

Prepare Lime Dressing. In a large bowl, combine lettuce, cucumber, tomato, onion, and coriander. Cut sausages diagonally into ¼-inch-thick slices (or thinly slice salami). Place meat and oil in a wide frying pan over low heat; cook, stirring occasionally, until meat is lightly browned. Add garlic and cook, stirring, just until golden. Add Lime Dressing; stir just until heated through. Pour over lettuce mixture and toss lightly. Serve immediately. Makes 4 first-course servings or 2 entrée servings.

Lime Dressing. In a small bowl, stir together ⅓ cup **lime juice**, 2½ tablespoons **sugar**, 1 tablespoon **fish sauce** or soy sauce, and ½ to ¾ teaspoon **crushed red pepper**.

Sesame-topped Vegetables

From Malaysia comes *Achar*, a colorful tumble of crisp sweet-and-sour vegetables. It provides a cooling contrast to any highly spiced entrée.

> ½ English or European cucumber
> 3 large carrots
> 3 cups cauliflowerets
> ½ cup sesame seeds
> ⅓ cup salad oil
> 2 cloves garlic, minced or pressed
> ½ cup minced shallots
> ½ cup white (distilled) vinegar
> ¼ cup sugar
> Soy sauce

Cut cucumber and carrots into thin slivers, 3 to 4 inches long. Break cauliflowerets into smaller flowerets. Set vegetables aside.

In a wide frying pan over medium heat, toast sesame seeds, shaking pan frequently, until golden (about 2 minutes); set aside.

Heat oil in pan over medium heat. Add garlic and shallots. Cook, stirring, until shallots are soft. Increase heat to high and add vinegar, sugar, cauliflowerets, and carrots. Cook, stirring, until vegetables are tender-crisp to bite; add cucumber and cook, stirring, until heated through. Season to taste with soy. Transfer to a rimmed serving plate; sprinkle with sesame seeds. Serve warm or at room temperature. Makes 6 to 8 servings.

Tomato & Onion Salad

This colorful salad from the Philippines is a suitable partner for any robust entrée. When fresh tomatoes are out of season, substitute slices of canned heart of palm.

> 1 mild white onion, sliced
> 12 cups water
> 1 tablespoon salt
> 2 large bunches spinach (about 2 lbs. *total*), stems removed
> 2 large tomatoes, sliced
> ½ cup palm vinegar or ¼ cup *each* white (distilled) vinegar and water
> 1½ tablespoons sugar
> Salt and pepper

In a bowl, combine onion, 4 cups of the water, and salt; let stand for about 30 minutes. Drain, rinse, and drain again.

Rinse spinach well. Pour remaining 8 cups water into a 4 to 5-quart kettle; bring to a boil over high heat. Add spinach and cook just until wilted (about

1 minute). Drain, rinse, and squeeze dry.

Arrange spinach on a rimmed serving plate; top with onion and tomatoes.

In a small bowl, stir together vinegar and sugar. Season to taste with salt and pepper; drizzle over salad. Makes 6 servings.

Sour Vegetables

Delicious served warm or at room temperature, Indonesian *sayur asam*—vegetables stewed with beef in a broth tangy with tamarind—makes a pleasing accompaniment for grilled meats such as satay.

½ cup tamarind liquid (page 81) or ¼ cup lemon
   juice
1 small onion, cut into chunks
1 clove garlic
1 cup plus 2 tablespoons water
3 cups regular-strength chicken broth
1 medium-size eggplant (1 to 1¼ lbs.), cut into
   2-inch chunks
1 bay leaf
2 teaspoons sugar
¼ teaspoon crushed red pepper
¼ pound green beans, ends removed, cut into
   2-inch pieces
2 or 3 ears corn, cut into 1½-inch lengths
¼ pound lean boneless beef (sirloin or top
   round), thinly sliced across the grain
½ medium-size head cabbage, cut into 2-inch
   chunks
   Lemon juice
   Salt

Prepare tamarind liquid, using ½ cup hot water and ¼ cup pulp. Set aside.

Place onion, garlic, and 2 tablespoons of the water in a blender or food processor; whirl until smooth. Pour remaining 1 cup water into a 5-quart kettle and bring to a boil over high heat. Add onion mixture; cover, reduce heat to low, and simmer for 10 minutes. Add broth, eggplant, bay leaf, sugar, and pepper; cover and simmer for 10 minutes.

Add beans, corn, beef, and tamarind liquid; simmer, covered, until tender-crisp to bite (2 to 3 more minutes). Discard bay leaf. Season to taste with lemon juice and salt. If made ahead, let cool; then cover and refrigerate for up to 4 hours. Bring to room temperature before serving, or heat over medium heat until warmed through. Makes 6 to 8 servings.

Vegetable Plate
with Peanut Sauce

Gado gado is an Indonesian dish of raw and lightly cooked vegetables blanketed with a peppery peanut sauce. Shrimp chips (*krupuk*) are the traditional accompaniment. Thin and transparent in the package, they become puffy and opaque when fried. (If they're not available, omit them.)

Peanut Sauce (page 92)
**About 18 small or 6 large shrimp chips
(optional; frying directions follow)**
1 **pound green beans, ends removed, cut into
   1-inch pieces**
3 **large thin-skinned potatoes (about 1 lb.
   total)**
⅓ **pound bean sprouts, coarsely chopped**
1 **medium-size cucumber, thinly sliced**
3 **cups finely shredded cabbage**
1 **large carrot, cut diagonally into thin slices**
3 **hard-cooked eggs**

Prepare Peanut Sauce and fry shrimp chips (if used); set aside. Into a 3-quart pan, pour water to a depth of 1 inch; bring to a boil over high heat. Add beans; cover, reduce heat to medium, and cook until tender-crisp to bite (about 5 minutes). Drain, rinse with cold water, and drain again. Pour water into pan to a depth of 2 inches; bring to a boil over high heat. Add potatoes; cover, reduce heat to medium, and cook until tender throughout when pierced (25 to 30 minutes). Drain, let cool, and slice thinly. If desired, blanch bean sprouts: half-fill pan with water, bring to a boil over high heat, add sprouts, and cook just until boil resumes. Drain, rinse with cold water, and drain again.

Arrange cucumber slices around outside edges of 6 salad plates. Mound cabbage in center of plates; distribute beans and bean sprouts over cabbage. Layer potato slices atop cucumber slices; arrange carrot slices decoratively over all. Cut eggs into wedges; arrange around edges of plates. Pass Peanut Sauce at the table to spoon over servings; offer shrimp chips alongside. Makes 6 servings.

Shrimp chips. Into a wok or wide, heavy pan, pour **salad oil** to a depth of 2 inches. Heat to 375° on a deep-frying thermometer. Add chips and fry (3 or 4 at a time for small, 1 at a time for large) until puffy and lightly browned (about 30 seconds for small, 1½ minutes for large). Remove and drain briefly on paper towels. If made ahead, package airtight and store until next day. Serve at room temperature.

Green Papaya Salad

In Laos or Thailand, this salad would be made with the native papaya—a softball-size fruit that's picked and eaten green, when its flesh is tart and crunchy. Green papaya is available in some Oriental markets; if you can't find it, substitute carrots.

    1   pound firm green papaya or carrots
    1   small dried whole hot red chile
    1   clove garlic
    1½ tablespoons lime juice
    1   tablespoon sugar
    1   tablespoon anchovy cream or fish sauce
        (optional)
    1   small tomato, cut into thin wedges
        Lime wedges
        Fresh coriander (cilantro) sprigs

Peel and seed papaya. Using a sharp knife, cut into long, thin shreds; or shred with a regular or Japanese-style shredder (you should have about 3 cups).

Using a mortar and pestle, pound chile and garlic until finely crushed (or chop very finely). Place in a serving bowl; stir in lime juice, sugar, and anchovy cream (if used). Stir in tomato and papaya. Garnish with lime and coriander. Makes 4 servings.

Marinated Cucumbers
(Pictured on front cover)

This simple condiment from Thailand provides a cooling counterpart to a spicy entrée.

    ⅓   cup white (distilled) vinegar
    ¼   cup *each* sugar and water
    ¼   teaspoon salt
    1   large cucumber
    ¼   cup chopped roasted peanuts (optional)

In a small pan, combine vinegar, sugar, water, and salt. Cook over medium heat, stirring, until liquid boils and sugar is dissolved; remove from heat and let cool to room temperature.

Peel or score cucumber, if desired. Cut lengthwise into quarters; then cut quarters crosswise into ⅛-inch-thick slices. Place in a serving bowl. Pour marinade over cucumbers; stir to blend. If made ahead, cover and refrigerate for up to 2 hours. Top with peanuts, if desired. Makes 4 to 6 servings.

Chili Paste
(Pictured on page 79)

Sambal is to Indonesian cuisine what salsa is to Mexican cooking: a fiery-hot condiment served at every meal.

    ½   cup small dried whole hot red chiles,
        stemmed and seeded
    2   cloves garlic, halved
    1   small onion, coarsely chopped
    ¼   cup *each* sugar, lemon juice, and water
    ½   teaspoon salt

In a blender or food processor, combine chiles, garlic, onion, sugar, lemon juice, water, and salt; whirl until onions are finely minced. Pour mixture into a 1 to 2-quart pan and cook over medium heat, stirring occasionally, until reduced to about ½ cup (about 10 minutes). Serve at room temperature. Makes about ½ cup.

Spiced Coconut
(Pictured on page 79)

Most Indonesian dinner tables are brightened by condiments—such as *serunding*, a sweet and toasty-tasting mixture of coconut, peanuts, and spices. Try it sprinkled over plain rice or Festive Yellow Rice (page 78).

    2   tablespoons salad oil
    1   small onion, finely chopped
    1   clove garlic, minced or pressed
    1   teaspoon ground coriander
    ½   teaspoon ground cumin
    1½ cups shredded unsweetened coconut
    ½   cup roasted unsalted peanuts (optional)
    2   tablespoons sugar
    1   tablespoon lemon juice
        Salt

Heat oil in a wide frying pan over medium heat. Add onion and garlic and cook, stirring, until soft. Reduce heat to medium-low and stir in coriander, cumin, coconut, peanuts (if used), sugar, and lemon juice; season to taste with salt. Cook, stirring often, until coconut is lightly browned (about 15 minutes). If made ahead, let cool, then cover and refrigerate for up to 2 weeks. Serve at room temperature. Makes 2 to 2½ cups.

ข้าว Desserts

Banana Fritters

Tender bites of batter-coated, deep-fried fruit are a favorite snack in Indonesia.

  2 large half-ripe (green-tipped) bananas
  ⅓ cup all-purpose flour
  3 tablespoons sugar
  2 tablespoons cornstarch
  ⅓ cup water
    Salad oil
    Granulated or brown sugar (optional)

Cut bananas crosswise into thirds; then cut each piece in half lengthwise. Combine flour, the 3 tablespoons sugar, and cornstarch. Add water; stir until smooth. Place fruit in batter; turn to coat.

Into a deep, heavy pan, pour oil to a depth of 1½ inches and heat to 350° on a deep-frying thermometer. Lift fruit, a piece at a time, from batter; let excess batter drip off. Lower fruit into oil. Cook, several pieces at a time, until lightly browned (about 1½ minutes). Remove with a slotted spoon; drain on paper towels. If desired, sprinkle with additional sugar; serve immediately. Makes 6 to 8 servings.

Sticky Rice with Mangoes

Succulent mangoes and sweet rice are topped with coconut cream in the Thai equivalent of rice pudding.

  3 cups fresh coconut milk (page 89)
  ⅔ cup sticky rice (also called glutinous or sweet rice)
  ¼ cup sugar
  ½ teaspoon salt
  2 large mangoes, peeled and cut into wedges

Prepare coconut milk. Cover and refrigerate for at least 2 hours or until next day; milk will separate into a top layer of cream and a bottom layer of milk. Skim off cream; place in a measuring cup and add some of the milk, if necessary, to make 1 cup total.

Rinse rice with cold water until water runs clear; then soak in water to cover for 2 hours. Drain. In top of a double boiler, scald remaining thin coconut milk (about 2 cups); add rice, sugar, and salt. Cover and cook over simmering water until rice is tender (15 to 20 minutes). Remove from heat; spoon into a serving bowl. Let cool to room temperature.

Divide mangoes among 4 individual plates. Spoon cooled rice alongside; pour ¼ cup of the coconut cream over each serving. Makes 4 servings.

Leche Flan

This rich, caramel-topped custard from the Philippines is sure to satisfy your sweet tooth.

  ½ cup sugar
  1 large can (13 oz.) evaporated milk
  ⅓ cup milk
  6 egg yolks
  3 eggs
  1 teaspoon vanilla
  1 tablespoon grated lime or lemon peel

Preheat oven to 350°. Make a hot water bath for flan: set a 1½-quart oval baking dish in a slightly larger pan. Hold baking dish down so it won't float and pour hot water into outer pan to a depth of 1½ inches. Remove dish from water; place pan in oven.

Place sugar in a small heavy pan over medium heat. As sugar begins to melt into syrup, tip pan and swirl melting sugar over bottom; continue until sugar is completely melted and syrup is a clear, medium amber color. Pour syrup into baking dish and, protecting your hands, tilt dish quickly so syrup coats bottom and about 1½ inches of sides. Set dish on a wire rack; caramel will harden quickly.

In a large bowl, combine evaporated milk, milk, egg yolks, eggs, vanilla, and lime peel; beat until well blended. Pour into caramel-lined dish; set in hot water bath in oven. Bake, uncovered, for 25 to 30 minutes or until a knife inserted just off center comes out clean. Remove dish from water bath; let cool, then cover and refrigerate for at least 8 hours or until next day. As flan cools, caramel liquefies. To unmold, run knife around edge of dish, then cover with a rimmed oval serving plate. Holding plate in place, quickly invert dish, turning out custard; caramel will collect at base.

To serve, cut into small squares or wedges; spoon caramel on top. Makes 8 to 10 servings.

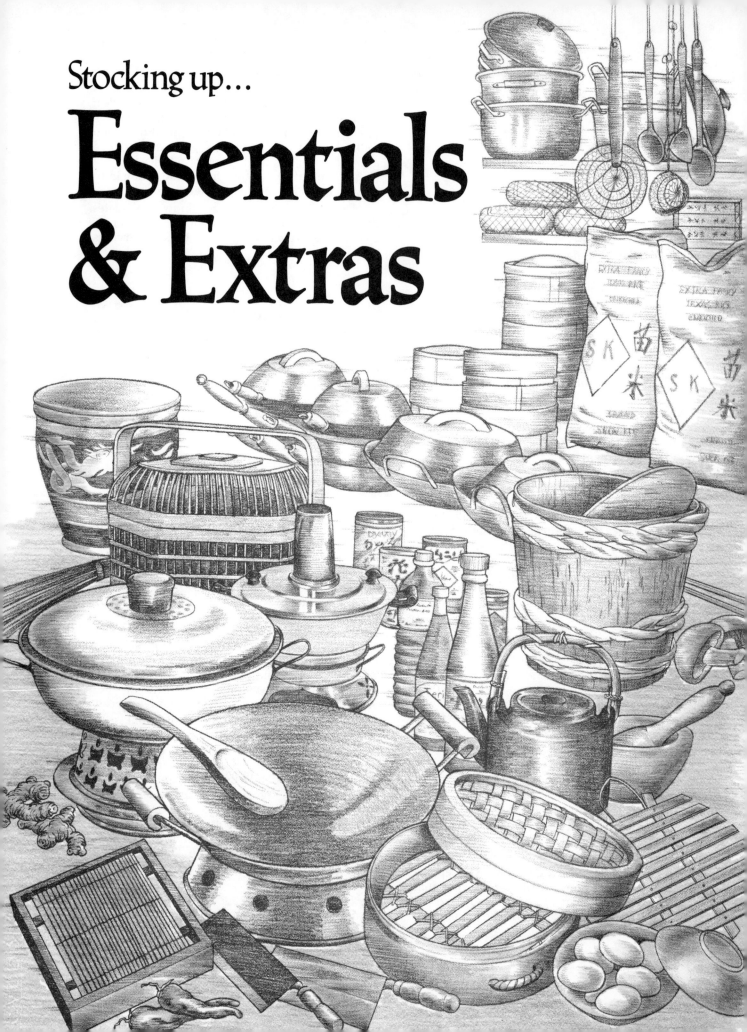

Stocking up...
Essentials & Extras

Part of the fun of exploring a new ethnic cuisine is learning about the unusual food products and kitchen tools available from that part of the world. Experimenting with a new spice or cooking technique will broaden your expertise and add variety to your menus.

At first glance, though, an Oriental market may seem more like an overwhelming maze of unfamiliar produce, packages, and gadgets than a place for discovery. To help clear up the confusion, fortify yourself with a bit of knowledge before you set out on a shopping excursion. Let the following information serve as a guide to what's available, how to use it, and even how to do without it.

Oriental shops offer a fascinating selection of cooking equipment and ingredients.

Kitchen Equipment

Like other ethnic cuisines, Oriental cooking has its own *batterie de cuisine:* woks, steamers, and hot pots replace the arsenal of pots and pans more familiar to Western cooks. You'll find it exciting to use these authentic utensils—but none of them is essential for success with recipes in this book.

Tools for Preparation

A sharp edge on a Chinese cleaver, a Japanese knife, or even a French chef's knife is the only prerequisite for successful Oriental cooking: cutting, slicing, and chopping are important techniques in all the cuisines of the region. Other cutting tools, such as a Japanese vegetable slicer, will also prove useful timesavers.

Chopping block. Traditional Chinese equipment; a round, thick board, traditionally cut from a tree trunk. Any sturdy cutting board can substitute.

Chinese cleavers. Available in 3 weights. Medium weight is best for all-purpose use—slicing, mincing, chopping, and hacking. The broad blade also serves as a scoop to transfer cut-up foods from board to wok. Many cleavers are made of carbon steel; dry these well after washing to prevent rusting.

Japanese knives. Distinguished by the fact that only one side of the blade has an edge. There are 3 basic shapes, each with a different function. Left to right: cleaver is for cutting seafood, poultry, and meat; it can cut through thin, lightweight bones. *Vegetable knife* is for slicing, chopping, and mincing vegetables. *Thin slicer for fish* has a long, thin blade for slicing delicate sashimi.

Decorative vegetable cutters. Used to make flower-shaped vegetable slices. Good for carrot and daikon.

Vegetable slicer (pictured on page 100). A versatile and inexpensive Japanese tool. Interchangeable and adjustable blades for slicing and coarse or fine shredding fit onto a plastic base.

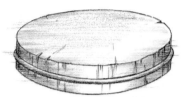

Chopping block

Chinese cleaver

Japanese knives

**Decorative
vegetable cutters**

**Japanese
vegetable slicer**

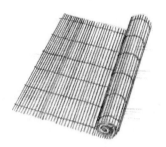

Bamboo mat

Small grater

**Mortar and
pestle**

Bamboo mat. Called *sudare* in Japanese; used for rolling sushi into neat cylinders (see page 43). A slatted bamboo placemat is a good substitute.

Small grater. Japanese tool made of aluminum or stainless steel; useful for grating ginger, daikon, and citrus peel.

Mortar and pestle. Used throughout the Orient to grind together spices and seasonings.

Suribachi with wooden pestle. Japanese mortar, traditionally used for grinding sesame seeds. Has a rough-sided interior that makes it easier to crush seeds into a paste.

Cooking Utensils

If you buy only one piece of cookware, we recommend the wok for its sheer versatility: you can use it to stir-fry, braise, steam, and deep-fry.

Wok. Of Chinese origin, the wok has counterparts all over Asia. Woks can be made from cast iron, carbon steel, aluminum, stainless steel, or copper; carbon steel is the most widely available material. (Carbon steel woks must be seasoned before using—see below.) Some woks come in sets including lids and rings. Lids are useful for stir-frying, steaming, and braising; rings stabilize the wok for use over a gas flame. (We recommend placing a flat-bottomed wok directly on the heat element of an electric range.)

If your wok is made of carbon steel (as many are), it must be seasoned before using. First wash it with sudsy water and rinse it. Then dry it on your range by placing it on range element directly over high heat for a minute or two. Next, rub inside of wok with a paper towel dipped in salad oil; remove any excess oil with another paper towel. After each use, wash wok and dry it on range element; if not kept entirely dry between uses, it will rust.

Wok tools. *Spatula:* long, wooden-handled tool designed to fit the curve of the wok and facilitate tossing while stir-frying. *Ladle:* another long, wooden-handled utensil, good for serving soups or spooning hot oil over foods while deep-frying. *Strainer:* ideal tool for lifting cooked foods from hot water or oil; has a long wooden handle attached to an oversize wire screen.

**Suribachi with
wooden pestle**

Wok

Spatula

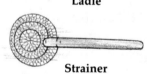

Ladle

Strainer

Electric wok

Bamboo steamer

Aluminum steamer

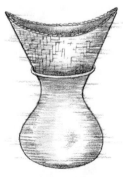

Rice steaming basket

Electric wok. Well suited to tabletop cooking; especially good for hot pot meals. Stir-frying in electric woks isn't always successful, since these woks recover heat rather slowly after food is added. (Add food in smaller batches to help maintain maximum heat.)

Bamboo steamer. Traditional Chinese utensil, with stacking bamboo sections and a bamboo lid; available in sizes ranging from 6 to 12 inches in diameter. The layered arrangement allows you to steam several dishes at once. Bamboo absorbs moisture, so steam doesn't condense on underside of lid. To use steamer, place it over boiling water in a wok or wide pan.

Aluminum steamer. A more modern steamer; like the bamboo variety, it's available in various sizes and composed of stacking sections topped with a lid. Bottom section holds boiling water. Place a towel beneath lid to absorb condensation.

Rice steaming basket. Capacious vessel used in Laos and northern Thailand for steaming sticky rice. The large basket fits over a tall hourglass-shaped pan that holds boiling water. For substitutes, see page 78.

Electric rice steamer. Rice cooks perfectly in conventional steamers and pans, but if you cook rice often, you may want to invest in this modern and convenient Japanese appliance.

Cooking chopsticks. Extra-long chopsticks (sometimes tied at the top), used during cooking to keep hands at safe distance from hot foods.

Hot pot (also called Mongolian hot pot). Used for tabletop cooking in China, Japan, Korea, and parts of Southeast Asia; consists of a cylindrical chimney surrounded by a moat in which food is cooked. Heated charcoal placed in the chimney keeps liquid in the moat hot. *Caution:* Use a hot pot only in a well-ventilated room. Do not add hot charcoal to chimney until moat is filled with liquid; otherwise, pot may melt. Be sure the pot you use is made from material suitable for cooking (some pots are purely decorative). In place of a hot pot, you may use a fondue pot, chafing dish, electric wok or frying pan, or a kettle over a portable tabletop cook unit.

Hot pot strainer. Small wire strainer shaped like a deep spoon, used for dipping foods into a hot pot.

Electric rice steamer

Cooking chopsticks

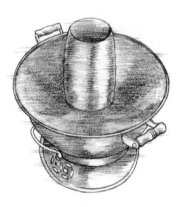

Hot pot

Hot pot strainer

Hibachi

Genghis Khan grill

Sukiyaki pan

Clay pot

Japanese clay pot (donabi)

Hibachi. Small Japanese grill. Especially suitable for barbecuing small pieces of meat—Barbecued Beef Strips (page 70) and Skewered Chicken (page 51), for example.

Genghis Khan grill. Dome-shaped grill (said to resemble Khan's helmet) with narrow slots for drainage. Meat cooks on top of dome; vegetables are placed along its side. Heat over low coals to use. Use of this grill spread to Japan and Korea from northern China (see Mongolian Grill, page 32).

Sukiyaki pan. Square or round shallow Japanese pan designed for tabletop cooking; made of heavy cast iron. Season as directed for wok (page 100). With the addition of a wire draining rack, it doubles as a tempura pan.

Clay pots. Bisque-colored Chinese pots (also called sandy pots) are unglazed; Japanese pots, called *donabi*, may be glazed (bottom is always unglazed). Donabi, always equipped with lids, are traditional vessels for dishes such as Simmered Shellfish (page 48).

Before using, soak both pot and lid in water for at least 24 hours. Then let dry for another 24 hours. No further soaking is necessary. (Newer Chinese pots may have different care requirements; follow manufacturer's instructions.) For cooking, place pot on a wire diffuser over an electric element, or place directly over gas flame. Never set a chilled pot on a hot burner, or a hot pot on a cold or wet surface; if you do, pot will crack.

Serving Dishes

There's no need to invest in a new set of tableware for serving Oriental meals. With nothing more than chopsticks and handleless teacups to accent Western plates and bowls, your table will take on an Oriental look.

The Japanese, with their tradition of impeccable presentation, have the most elaborate collection of serving pieces. These are easy to improvise, however; you need only substitute a dish matching the genuine article in basic size and function.

Southeast Asian cooks—in contrast to the Japanese—use very few special serving dishes. You can create an appropriately tropical look for your meal simply by serving food in large, flat baskets lined with banana, fig, or ti leaves (see page 104).

Chinese soup bowl

Japanese soup bowl

Korean soup bowl

Chinese rice bowl

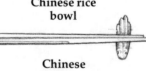

Chinese chopsticks

Japanese rice bowl

Japanese chopsticks

Korean rice bowl

Korean chopsticks

Southeast Asian rice basket

Chinese soup bowl. Small porcelain bowl holds a single serving of soup; can also be used for rice.

Japanese soup bowl. Small, lidded lacquer bowl for serving simple soups such as Miso Soup (page 41). You can use it for rice, too.

Korean soup bowl. Wide, fairly shallow bowl for hearty soups; usually made of earthenware.

Chinese rice bowl. Porcelain bowl that serves as a "dinner plate" at Chinese family-style meals. Portions of various dishes are placed on rice; diners eat foods first, then rice, flavored with sauces absorbed from each dish.

Chinese chopsticks. Blunt-ended chopsticks made of wood, bamboo, lacquer, plastic, or (rarely) more precious materials such as ivory.

Japanese rice bowl. Lidded lacquer bowl; shaped like a Japanese soup bowl. In Japan, rice is usually eaten separately, as an accompaniment to (not a base for) other dishes.

Japanese chopsticks. Made of the same materials as Chinese chopsticks, but a little shorter, and pointed at the tips.

Korean rice bowl. Made of stainless steel (or silver); like a Chinese rice bowl, it's used as a "dinner plate" at family meals.

Korean chopsticks. Made of stainless steel (or silver); short and blunt tipped.

Southeast Asian rice basket. A small, lidded basket, used in Laos and northern Thailand for serving sticky rice. Substitute any small basket.

Sushi plate. Small rectangular dish (with or without rim) for serving individual portions of sushi (pages 43–44) and sashimi (page 49).

Small vegetable plate. Japanese serving dish for individual portions of condiments or vegetables.

Donburi bowl. Shaped like a Japanese rice bowl, but larger. Donburi (page 50) is one of the few Japanese dishes that's always served over rice.

Chinese pedestal platter. Often used to serve stir-fried dishes.

Chinese platter. Best for serving dishes that don't have much sauce, such as Tea-smoked Duck (page 30) and Red-cooked Chicken (page 29).

Sushi plate

Small vegetable plate

Donburi bowl

Chinese pedestal platter

Chinese platter

A Glossary of Ingredients

If you're puzzled at the sight of six brands of soy sauce or four brands of rice lined up on a shelf, take heart. It's a subject that's perplexing to many. What follows is a short primer intended to help guide you through the aisles of an Oriental market. Information on selection, storage, and use will help simplify a sticky subject.

Rice, Noodles & Wrappers

Bean threads. These thin, near-transparent strands are made from ground mung beans. They're also sold as *harusame* (their Japanese name) and as cellophane, translucent, and shining noodles. Widely used in Japan, China, and Southeast Asia, they have a neutral flavor and readily absorb flavors from other foods. Simply soaked and heated through, they have a slippery texture. They can also be deep-fried as directed for thin rice noodles (see page 81).

Uncooked bean threads will keep indefinitely if stored in a cool, dry place. Before using, soak in warm water until pliable (about 30 minutes).

Chinese noodles. A staple in the north of China, these wheat-flour noodles may or may not contain eggs. Sometimes labeled as *mein* (their Chinese name), they're available both fresh and dried, in packages of looped or curly bundles. Use fresh noodles within a day or two, or freeze for longer storage; dried mein will keep indefinitely if stored in a cool, dry place. You can use any fresh or dried thin noodles or spaghetti in place of mein.

Egg roll skins. Rectangular flour-and-egg wrappers for Chinese fried pastries exist in several forms. The Cantonese version is called an *egg roll skin* (or wrapper); *spring roll skins*, from Shanghai, are a thinner type that give a crisper and more delicate crust after frying. You'll find egg roll skins in Oriental markets and most supermarkets. Refrigerate for up to a few days, or freeze for longer storage.

Gyoza. These round wrappers made from flour and water are used to make Pot Stickers (page 15). You can buy *gyoza* in Oriental markets and well-stocked supermarkets. Unopened, they'll keep in the refrigerator for up to 3 weeks; once opened, they should be used within a few days.

Leaves. In Southeast Asia, leaves are often used to line serving baskets and to wrap food for carrying (unlike dough wrappers, these aren't intended to form edible jackets for a filling). You can use any decorative, nonpoisonous leaves.

Ti leaves (pictured on page 74) are readily available from florists in the United States. *Banana leaves* (pictured on page 87) are sold frozen in 1-pound packages; look for them in Latin American and Oriental markets.

Thaw banana leaves before using, then rinse and pat dry. Glide flat surface of leaves across gas flame or electric element on highest heat setting. In just a few seconds, leaves will become shiny and pliable, and give off a pleasant aroma. Set aside until ready to use (up to several hours). Return any unprepared leaves to freezer; store for up to several months.

Long-grain rice. In China and much of Southeast Asia, long-grain rice is preferred over other varieties. See page 21 for steaming instructions.

Lumpia wrappers. The Filipino version of the egg roll is based on these thin pancakes. Made sometimes from a simple flour-and-water dough, sometimes from cornstarch, eggs, and water, the pancakes are sold, frozen, in Oriental markets. They'll keep for about 6 months in the freezer.

Thin rice noodles. As the name indicates, these noodles (also called rice sticks and *mai fun*) are slender strands made from rice flour. A common ingredient throughout Asia, they're available in Oriental markets. Rice noodles are tasty in soups and stir-fries; boil them before using, or soak in warm water until pliable. (Because thickness varies from brand to brand, soaking time ranges from 20 to 30 minutes.) You can also deep-fry the noodles to make a crunchy garnish (see page 81). Uncooked noodles will keep indefinitely in a cool, dry place.

Rice paper. Spread thin on bamboo trays, a mixture of rice flour and water dries into translucent, papery sheets. When deep-fried (as in Imperial Rolls, page 75), rice paper wrappers become delicately crisp. You can also use them straight from the package; after moistening with water, they'll be ready to fill and fold (see page 90). You can buy rice paper in rounds or triangles of varying size and thickness; in general, the thinner the paper, the better it tastes. Left unopened and stored in a cool, dry place, packaged rice paper keeps indefinitely.

Shirataki. These soft, translucent noodles are made from a taro-like tuber called "devil's tongue." Like bean threads, they readily soak up other flavors. Also called boiled yam noodles and alimentary paste, *shirataki* are sold in cans or plastic tubs; look for them in Oriental markets.

Short-grain rice. Japanese cooks favor short-grain rice for almost every use. Cooked the Japanese way (page 44), it's slightly sticky, making it easy to manage with chopsticks. Often called pearl rice, it's also the staple grain in Korea and the Philippines. Look for the names Calrose, Blue Rose, or Kokuho Rose on the package. (You may substitute medium-grain rice; cook as directed for short-grain rice.)

Sticky rice. Look for sticky rice—also called glutinous, sweet, and *mochi* rice—in Oriental markets. It has a sticky texture and a slightly sweet flavor when cooked. Sticky rice is a popular base for desserts in China and Japan; in Laos and northern Thailand, it's the favorite for every use. See page 78 for steaming instructions.

Soba. Buckwheat flour tints these slender Japanese noodles a dull gray brown; you may also see green *soba*, tinted with green tea. Usually sold dried, the noodles are sometimes available fresh in Japanese markets. *Chuka soba* are quick-cooking wheat-flour noodles; several varieties exist.

Somen. These fine Japanese noodles are usually produced from hard wheat flour mixed with oil. Most *somen* are white, but you'll sometimes see a yellow variety that contains egg yolk. Stored in a cool, dry place, dried somen will keep almost indefinitely.

Udon. Resembling square spaghetti, these thick wheat-flour noodles are usually sold dried. (Occasionally, though, you'll find fresh ones in Japanese markets; they freeze beautifully.) Like any dried pasta, dried udon will keep almost indefinitely if stored in a cool, dry place.

Won ton skins. You can buy won ton skins (or wrappers) in Oriental markets and in most supermarkets. Store them (wrapped airtight) in the refrigerator for up to a week, in the freezer for several months.

Herbs, Spices & Seasonings

Black beans. Small fermented black beans preserved in salt are used to flavor Chinese sauces. They're sold in small jars or plastic bags in three styles: plain, flavored with garlic, and flavored with ginger. Store them in a tightly covered jar in a cool, dry place; rinse them thoroughly with water before using.

Chiles. The spicy dishes enjoyed in many Asian countries get their hot, nippy flavor from chiles—fresh, dried, or pickled.

Asian varieties of *fresh chiles* are difficult to find in the United States;

just substitute jalapeño or other hot green, red, or yellow chiles. (You may also used dried, canned, or pickled chiles in place of fresh.) Before chopping fresh chiles, remove the seeds and veins—the two hottest portions. Since the chile's potent oils can sting bare skin, wear rubber gloves when you perform this operation. After handling chiles, keep fingers away from your face (especially eyes).

The *dried chiles* generally used in China and Southeast Asia are small (1 to 2 inches long) and fiery hot; in Thailand, they're called "bird's eye chiles." Both Oriental and Latin American markets carry dried whole chiles. If you wish, you may substitute crushed red pepper; allow ¼ teaspoon for each chile.

Pickled hot chiles—chiles pickled in vinegar, sugar, and salt—are a nippy-hot Southeast Asian condiment. They're typically used to add a little heat to mild cooked foods. In Southeast Asia, the chiles are usually pickled at home; in the U.S., you'll find them in jars in Oriental markets.

Chinese five-spice. Bottled by American and Asian spice companies and widely available, Chinese five-spice is a blend of ground cloves, fennel, licorice root, cinnamon, and star anise.

Chinese mustard. Spicy-hot Chinese mustard is sold in jars and used as a dip for meats, seafood, and savory pastries. You can make your own (see page 16).

Citrus leaves. Dried leaves of the wild lime tree, packaged whole or powdered, flavor curry dishes of Thailand, Malaysia, and Indonesia. You'll find this seasoning in Oriental markets; store it in an airtight container in a cool, dry place. For each leaf, you may substitute ¼ teaspoon powder.

Coriander. Also called cilantro and Chinese parsley, this nippy and aromatic herb is used for seasoning and garnishing. It's sold by the bunch in Oriental markets and most supermarkets. After purchasing fresh coriander, rinse it and shake off excess water; then wrap in paper towels, place in a plastic bag, and refrigerate. Use within 1 week.

Curry paste. Cooks in Thailand still pound their curry spices into a paste with a mortar and pestle, but a more convenient alternative is available in the United States. Thai curry pastes are sold in packets, cans, and bags in markets that specialize in Southeast Asian products. In general, yellow paste is the mildest, green the hottest; orange and red are in between.

Curry powder. This favorite Indian flavoring is also extensively used in Southeast Asian cooking. Asian cooks prepare their own curry powder daily in small batches; in the United States, commercial blends are available. Curry powder typically contains some combination of turmeric, coriander, cloves, cardamom, ginger, mace, red and black pepper, and other spices. Store in a cool, dark place; heat, light, and humidity cause it to deteriorate rapidly.

Galangal. A first cousin to ginger, galangal is an important seasoning in Southeast Asian cooking, used to flavor curries, soups, and stews. Though the fresh root is unavailable in the United States, you will find dry galangal, both in slices and powdered form. It may be labeled as *laos* (its Indonesian name). Crush dry galangal slices finely before using in smooth-textured mixtures; leave whole for infusing flavor into simmered dishes.

Ginger. Aromatic ginger is a popular seasoning in Oriental cooking. The khaki colored *fresh ginger* sold in American markets is usually mature ginger imported from Hawaii or Jamaica. (Roots with dry, wrinkled skin are overmature and have a dry, fibrous texture; don't buy them.) In summer, you may see young ginger. Its skin is blondish, almost identical in color to the crisp ivory interior, and rosy shoots sprout from its gnarled sides. Young ginger is more tender and less pungent than mature roots, so you can use more of it.

Peel mature ginger, if desired. Wrapped in plastic wrap and stored in the refrigerator, fresh ginger keeps about 2 weeks. You can freeze ginger for up to several months, but its texture will suffer.

Pickled ginger is a popular garnish and relish in both Japan and China.

Japan's pickled red or pink ginger (*shoga*) comes in small jars; it's typically served with sushi. Chinese pickled ginger is usually enjoyed with sweet-and-sour dishes. Both types will keep for several months in the refrigerator.

Preserved ginger, packed in red syrup, is sweet and pungent. In Oriental markets, you may see it packaged in porcelain jars. Chinese cooks use it sparingly to season chicken and fish; it's also delicious used as a dessert topping. It keeps well at room temperature; if you refrigerate it, the syrup may crystallize.

Korean red pepper. This fiery spice looks like ground red pepper (cayenne), but it's made from a different chile and has a coarser grind. Cayenne is a good substitute.

Lemon grass. A Southeast Asian favorite, citrus-scented lemon grass adds distinctive flavor and aroma to the cooking of Indonesia, Malaysia, Indochina, and Thailand. Its long, woody stalk grows from a base that resembles the white part of a green onion. Though it's occasionally sold fresh in Oriental markets, you're more likely to find it frozen (in whole stalks) and dried. Dried lemon grass is available both as a powder (sometimes labeled as *sereh*) and in whole or sliced stalks; the sliced form is often sold as tea in herb and natural food shops.

If you get the chance to buy fresh lemon grass, choose the freshest possible stalks. Place in a plastic bag and store in the refrigerator; use within 6 weeks. Just before using, crush it lightly to release flavor. If you plan to slice the lemon grass or use it in a smooth-textured mixture (such as a curry paste), use only the white base up to the first branch off the stalk. (For other purposes—infusing flavor into broth, for example—use the entire stalk.) For 1 stalk fresh or dry lemon grass, you may substitute 1 teaspoon powdered lemon grass, ¼ cup sliced dry lemon grass, or the yellow part of peel from 1 lemon.

Shrimp. Added in minute quantities to a variety of dishes, tiny dried shrimp are a favorite flavoring in the Orient. Shelled, salted, and dried before packaging, they must be soaked in warm water for about 30 minutes before using. Stored airtight in a cool, dry place, they'll keep indefinitely.

Star anise. Shaped like an eight-pointed star, this aromatic seed pod has a strong licorice flavor. In Oriental markets and spice shops, you'll find it sold by weight. Store airtight at room temperature. If you can't find it, substitute 1 teaspoon anise seeds for each whole pod.

Szechwan peppercorns. These tiny reddish brown peppercorns have a mildly hot flavor and a pleasantly pungent aroma. Buy them in cellophane packages in Oriental markets. Before using peppercorns, dry-roast to bring out flavor (see page 30).

Tamarind. Tamarind is the fruit of a Southeast Asian legume. Oriental markets display it in various forms: whole pods, powder, bricks (choose the softest), and jars of prepared pulp. Left unopened, packaged pods, powder, and pulp will keep indefinitely at room temperature. Once opened, they'll stay fresh for a few weeks in the refrigerator, for several months in the freezer. To make the sour tamarind liquid used to flavor sauces, you'll need to soak the pulp (see page 81).

Tangerine peel. Used sparingly by Chinese cooks as both a seasoning and a garnish, dried tangerine peel is sold in strips in small cellophane packages. The peel is usually chopped for use in cooking, but sometimes a strip is left whole in a simmered dish and removed before serving. Before using peel, soak it in warm water for 20 minutes; discard white membrane.

Wasabi. Though this pungent root tastes something like horseradish, the two are in fact botanically unrelated. Finely grated wasabi root lends an extremely strong, sharp flavor to raw fish dishes such as sushi and sashimi. You won't find the fresh root in American markets, but it is available here in paste and powdered form. The ready-to-use paste, packaged in a tube, keeps in the refrigerator for several weeks. The green powder comes in a small can; to use it, mix with warm water to form a paste (see page 43).

Dried Products

Black fungus. Also called cloud or tree ears, these small, crinkly dried fungi are sold by weight in Oriental markets. Black fungus is a typical ingredient in Chinese and Southeast Asian cooking. Stored in a cool, dry place, it will keep indefinitely. Soak in warm water before using (the "ears" will expand dramatically).

Dashi. The clear, light broth called *dashi* lends characteristically Japanese flavor to soups, dipping sauces, and simmered dishes. You can make your own dashi by simmering *katsuobushi* and *kombu* (below) briefly in water, but we recommend a simple and speedy alternative: *dashi-no-moto*. This instant stock is available in granules and tea-bag-like bags; prepare according to package directions. Regular-strength chicken broth (skimmed of fat) is an acceptable substitute for dashi, though its flavor isn't as subtle.

Katsuobushi. Basic to dashi is the dried, flaked bonito called *katsuobushi*. In the United States, you'll find a bonito product called flower bonito or dried bonito flakes. Though not identical to katsuobushi, these flakes make acceptable dashi. Store airtight for up to 6 months.

Kombu. Along with katsuobushi, *kombu*—dried tangle seaweed—forms the base of dashi. Harvested off the shores of Hokkaido, Japan's northernmost island, the speckled brown seaweed is dried and cut into strips before packaging.

Nori. Best known as a sushi wrapper, *nori* (dried laver seaweed) is sold in sheets or strips. Japanese and Korean cooks also use this dark brown or green seaweed as a garnish. Cultivated in shallow coastal waters, it's dried (and sometimes roasted and seasoned with soy) before packaging. *Aonori,* prepared shredded seaweed sold in shaker-top bottles, is used as a garnish.

Oriental mushrooms. Shiitake mushrooms are used fresh (page 108) and dried. The dark dried mushrooms are widely available in small cellophane packages. Soak in warm water before using.

Pan ko. The Japanese use these coarse bread crumbs to give deep-fried foods a crunchy coating. Purchase them in Oriental markets, or make your own from the recipe on page 55.

Shrimp chips. Made of dried shrimp, egg whites, and tapioca, these chips (called *krupuk* in Indonesia) are common fare in Southeast Asia. You can buy Indonesian krupuk in both large and small sizes; the large chips have a more pronounced shrimp flavor. You'll need to deep-fry krupuk before serving them (see page 95). Left unopened and stored in a dry place, packaged shrimp chips will stay fresh for several months at room temperature. Deep-fried chips will keep in an airtight container for a day or two.

Tiger lily buds. Also called lily buds and golden needles, these pale gold, 2 to 3-inch-long dried buds are used in Chinese stir-fries and soups. They're sold by weight in Oriental markets.

 **Prepared Sauces & Flavorings**

Anchovy cream. Though the name may sound intriguing, the truth is that this blend of fermented anchovies and salt is a little too potently fishy, in both flavor and odor, to appeal to most Westerners. Anchovy cream is used as a seasoning in Indochinese cooking; you may find it labeled as *padek* (its Lao name). Be sure to store it in the refrigerator after opening.

Bean sauce. This thick brown sauce is made from fermented soybeans, salt, flour, and sugar. You'll find it sold under a variety of names, including yellow bean sauce, Chinese bean sauce, and brown bean sauce. Packaged in cans or jars, it's available in two forms: regular, which contains whole beans, and ground, which has a fairly smooth texture. Keep refrigerated (in a jar) after opening.

Sweet bean sauce is used in Szechwan-style cooking. If you can't find it, substitute hoisin sauce (below).

A *hot bean sauce* is also available. This spicy concoction is used sparingly in cooking or as a dipping sauce. Store (in a jar) in the refrigerator for up to 3 months. You can substitute 1 small dried whole hot red chile, crushed, for each teaspoon of hot bean sauce.

Coconut milk. For a complete discussion, see page 89.

Fish sauce. Thin, salty, brownish gray fish sauce is an all-purpose seasoning in Southeast Asia; it's popular in parts of China, as well. You may see it labeled as fish soy or fish's gravy. Both the Vietnamese version (*nuoc mam*) and the Burmese type are extremely strong flavored, and their aroma may overwhelm those unaccustomed to the frankly fishy bouquet. (The odor vanishes upon cooking, though.) Thai and Filipino fish sauces (*nam pla* and *patis*) are much milder. They're used as table condiments and in cooking. Store airtight in the refrigerator for up to several months.

Hoisin sauce. Spicy and slightly sweet, hoisin sauce is made from soybeans blended with flour, sugar, vinegar, and spices. Chinese cooks use this thick brownish red sauce both in cooking and as a condiment. You can buy hoisin in cans or jars; transfer canned sauce to an airtight jar after opening. The sauce keeps for several months in the refrigerator.

Kim chee. For a complete discussion, see page 65.

Korean hot red pepper paste. Koreans dab this salty, fiery-hot condiment on cooked foods to add hot, nippy flavor. The paste is sold in jars; after opening, store in the refrigerator for up to several months.

Mirin. This sweet rice wine is a basic Japanese flavoring ingredient. It adds subtle sweetness to a wide variety of dishes. You may substitute 1 tablespoon cream sherry or 1 teaspoon sugar for each tablespoon mirin.

Miso. Japan's *miso* is made from fermented soybeans mixed with crushed grain. Two types are commonly available. *White miso* is made with rice. *Red miso*, made with barley, is much saltier than the white variety. Miso is sold in plastic tubs in refrigerated foods sections (or on shelves) of Oriental markets. Refrigerate, airtight, for up to 3 months.

Oyster sauce. This thick brown sauce adds a subtle oyster flavor to stir-fried dishes. It's sold in bottles in Oriental markets and well-stocked supermarkets. Refrigerate after opening (it keeps for up to several months).

Plum sauce. Used for dipping and often served with duck, amber brown plum sauce is made with plums (or apricots), chiles, sugar, vinegar, and spices. It's available in jars or cans; after opening, refrigerate (in a jar) for up to several months.

Sake. For a complete discussion, see page 55.

Sambal. Indonesia's fiery-hot chili paste is used as a table condiment. You can make *sambal* from the recipe on page 96; it's also available, packed in jars, in Oriental markets that specialize in Southeast Asian products.

Shrimp paste. Several types of shrimp paste are sold in Oriental markets. Use the salty, grayish pink Chinese version sparingly as a flavoring in Chinese pork, poultry, vegetable, and rice dishes. Southeast Asian shrimp pastes, available in both fresh and dried forms, flavor sauces in the cooking of Burma (*ngasi*), Vietnam (*mam ruoc*), Malaysia (*blachan*), and Indonesia (*trasi*). The fresh paste is a pink liquid packaged in bottles and jars; store it in the refrigerator after opening (it will keep for several months). Dried shrimp paste will also keep for several months in a cool, dry place.

Soy sauce. Dark, savory, and salty, soy sauce is one of the most versatile and frequently used seasonings in Oriental cooking. It's made from soybeans, flour, yeast, salt, and sugar. Imported brands taste the best; saltiness varies from brand to brand.

Chinese cooks use three kinds of soy: light (the thinnest), dark (sweetened with caramel), and black (flavored with molasses). Added to dishes singly or in combination, these sauces produce a range of different flavorings.

Japanese soy is essentially a cross between the light and dark Chinese sauces (it's slightly sweeter than Chinese light soy). It's the most commonly available type, and may be used in cooking with good results: we've used it in preparing the recipes in this book. Indonesian soy is called *ketjap asin*—in place of it, you may use Chinese black soy.

Tientsin preserved vegetables. Like Korean *kim chee* (page 65), this Cantonese condiment is a combination of salted cabbage and seasonings. Also called *chong choy*, it's sometimes sold in pottery crocks (look for it in Oriental markets).

Tonkatsu sauce. This blend of Worcestershire, catsup, and soy sauce typically accompanies Japanese pork cutlet (*tonkatsu*). Buy the sauce in an Oriental market or a well-stocked supermarket, or make your own (see page 55).

 **Fresh Vegetables**

Bamboo shoots. The crunchy shoots of the tropical bamboo, eaten fresh in the Orient, are usually only available canned in the United States. You'll find both whole and sliced varieties. After opening rinse well; then cover with cold water and refrigerate for up to 10 days (change water daily).

Bean sprouts. Widely used in Oriental cooking, crisp soy or mung bean sprouts appear in supermarkets and Oriental markets. Choose short, plump, white sprouts. Refrigerate in a plastic bag for up to 4 days.

Bok choy. Sometimes called Chinese chard or white mustard cabbage, this elongated cabbage unfurls dark green leaves from long white stalks. Choose heads with smooth white stalks and crisp, unblemished leaves. Refrigerate in a plastic bag for up to 4 days.

Daikon. This white-fleshed root may grow as long as 14 inches and weigh a hefty 4 to 5 pounds. Japanese cooks simmer daikon in soups, preserve it in pungent pickles, and serve it raw (finely shredded, it's the classic garnish for sushi and sashimi). Look for daikon in Oriental markets and well-stocked supermarkets; choose smooth, firm roots that are free from any odor. Western white radishes are an acceptable substitute for raw daikon; use small turnips in place of daikon that's to be simmered.

Edible-pod peas. Also called Chinese pea pods, snow peas, and sugar peas, this vegetable is available fresh all year. (You can buy frozen peas, too, but they have a soft texture.) Choose small, crisp peas; refrigerate in a plastic bag for up to 4 days. Before cooking, break off tips; pull strings straight down pod sides.

Gobo. This slender root, also known as burdock, has brown skin and crisp, delicious white flesh. Popular in Japanese cooking, it's available fresh in Oriental markets. Choose young, tender roots less than an inch in diameter. (Avoid canned gobo—it's disappointing.) Don't wash the root, even if there's soil clinging to it, until just before using. Wrap in a paper bag and refrigerate for up to a few days.

Lotus root. Smooth-skinned lotus root grows in sections that resemble sausage links. Look for the fresh root in Chinese markets from midsummer through winter; ivory or brown in color, it's crisp textured and slightly sweet. Choose firm, unblemished roots. Wrap uncut lotus root in plastic wrap and refrigerate for up to 3 weeks.

Cut lotus root discolors quickly when exposed to air; to prevent this, drop pieces into cold water as you slice them.

Melon. Greenish yellow, bumpy-skinned *bitter melon* gets its slightly bitter taste from quinine. It's most often used in soups and stir-fries; look for it in Oriental markets from spring through summer. Store in the refrigerator for up to a week.

Bland-tasting *fuzzy melon* turns up in Cantonese soups, stir-fries, and braised dishes. The cylindrical green or yellow melon is in season during the summer; you may find it sold as hairy melon. It stays fresh for about 2 weeks if stored in the refrigerator.

Mushrooms. *Enoki mushrooms,* sometimes called *enokidake* or *enokitake,* have recently become a rather fashionable food in the United States. These cream colored Japanese mushrooms wear tiny round caps atop slender stalks up to 5 inches long. They're sold in small plastic bags in Japanese markets (as well as in some supermarkets). Refrigerate (unrinsed) in a plastic bag for up to a week. Because their flavor is so delicate, they're best eaten raw or lightly cooked; trim and discard dry, shriveled ends before using.

Grayish or tan *oyster mushrooms,* another Japanese favorite, grow in small clusters. You can buy them fresh in Oriental markets and some well-stocked supermarkets. Raw oyster mushrooms have a disagreeable taste; lightly cooked, they have a mild flavor and succulent texture.

Large, deep brown *shiitake mushrooms* have recently become available in some Oriental markets and supermarkets. Choose thick mushrooms whose caps are slightly curled under at the edges. Dried shiitake mushrooms (page 107) are widely available, but fresh ones have a more succulent texture. You can substitute button mushrooms for shiitake.

Napa cabbage. Sweet, mild-tasting napa cabbage is a favorite throughout the Orient. Also called Chinese cabbage and celery cabbage, it grows in a compact head shaped something like a head of romaine lettuce. Wrap in plastic wrap; refrigerate up to a week.

Oriental eggplant. In summer and early autumn, you may see these 4 to 8-inch-long eggplant in supermarkets and Oriental markets; they're often sold as Japanese eggplant. The flavor is sweeter and more pronounced than that of the larger Western eggplant. Oriental eggplant are well suited to a variety of cooking methods; try them deep-fried, stir-fried, grilled, or braised.

Water chestnuts. The tubers of a marsh plant, water chestnuts have a pleasingly crisp texture and a mildly sweet flavor. Widely available canned, they're also sold fresh in Chinese markets. Store them in a cool spot for up to a week; peel just before using, placing in water to prevent discoloring.

Canned water chestnuts are available both whole and sliced. After opening, rinse well; then cover with cold water, and refrigerate for up to 2 weeks (change water daily).

Yard-long beans. China's green beans may reach 2 feet in length; chopped into short pieces, they join many a stir-fry. In autumn, you may see the skinny pliable pods in Chinese and Caribbean markets. To store, wrap unrinsed beans in plastic wrap and refrigerate; use within a week.

Oils & Vinegars

Chili oil. Watch out: this orange red oil can be extremely hot. Sold in dispenser bottles, chili oil typically fires up stir-fry recipes; it's also served as a condiment.

Palm vinegar. Mild, cloudy-looking palm vinegar leaves an intensely sour aftertaste. It's available in Filipino markets. If you can't find it, substitute equal parts white (distilled) vinegar and water.

Rice vinegar. Japan's relatively mild rice vinegar is the type you're most likely to see in supermarkets and Oriental markets. Both seasoned and unseasoned types are available. Seasoned vinegar contains added sugar and salt; you can approximate its flavor by adding about 2 teaspoons sugar and salt to taste to every ¼ cup unseasoned vinegar.

Chinese rice vinegar—white, red, or black—has a stronger flavor than Japanese vinegar. If you can't find it, substitute red or white wine vinegar or Japanese rice vinegar.

Sesame oil. Golden brown and aromatic, this seasoning oil of China, Japan, and Korea is pressed from toasted sesame seeds. Since it's strong, use it sparingly.

Bean Curd, Eggs, Seafood & Meat

Abalone. Canned abalone is a good substitute for the fresh abalone enjoyed in China. Marinate and serve as a salad (page 17), or use thin slices as a garnish for stir-fries. Heat canned abalone just long enough to heat through; if overcooked, it will toughen.

Bean curd. This high-protein food is made from soybeans—soaked, cooked, and puréed, then coagulated into curd with epsom salts and vinegar. The custardy cakes, packed in water in plastic tubs, come in soft, medium-firm, and firm consistencies. (Bean curd labeled "regular" has a medium-firm consistency.) Though quite bland on its own, bean curd readily absorbs the flavors of other foods, making it a useful extender. Rinse packaged curd after opening; then cover with cold water and refrigerate for up to a few days (change water daily).

Fermented bean curd. Made from fermented soybeans mixed with crushed grain, this bean curd comes in two versions: white and red. The white type has a strong, salty, cheesy flavor; the red is somewhat milder, though still pungent. Stored airtight, both types keep in the refrigerator for up to 3 months. Serve as a condiment or toss with cooked vegetables.

Fried bean curd. Available in small pouches and cubes, fried bean curd is a popular addition to Chinese and Indonesian vegetable dishes. In Japan, the pouches are popular for making a kind of sushi in which the fried bean curd is stuffed with rice and other ingredients.

Kamaboko. This Japanese fish paste consists of puréed white fish mixed with potato starch and salt, then steamed. *Kamaboko* is ready to eat straight from the package; you'll find it in logs, cakes, and loaves, sometimes tinted bright pink around the edges.

Lop cheong. China's pork sausages come in 6-inch-long links. Before eating, steam for about 15 minutes; then serve with rice and a mustard dipping sauce. Or slice and stir-fry with other ingredients. Refrigerate for up to 1 month; freeze for longer storage.

Quail eggs. Tiny quail eggs, considered a delicacy in the Orient, taste much like hen's eggs; they're sold both raw and cooked. Store in the refrigerator for up to 2 weeks.

Salted duck eggs. Enjoyed in China and the Philippines, these eggs are cured in brine for a month before being sold. Both whites and yolks are very salty. Simmer raw eggs for about 1 hour before eating, changing water several times to reduce saltiness. Raw or cooked, the eggs keep in the refrigerator for up to 1 month.

Thousand-year-old eggs. These famous Chinese delicacies (made with duck eggs) are cured for about 100 days in a mixture of lime, ashes, tea, and salt. They have amber colored whites, green yolks, and a pungent flavor. Before serving, soak in cold water for about an hour to soften the black coating; then scrape it off with a knife. Wrapped airtight and stored in the refrigerator, peeled eggs will keep for up to 1 month.

Index

Metric Conversion Table

To change	To	Multiply by
ounces (oz.)	grams (g)	28
pounds (lbs.)	kilograms (kg)	0.45
teaspoons	milliliters (ml)	5
tablespoons	milliliters (ml)	15
fluid ounces (fl. oz.)	milliliters (ml)	30
cups	liters (l)	0.24
pints (pt.)	liters (l)	0.47
quarts (qt.)	liters (l)	0.95
gallons (gal.)	liters (l)	3.8
Fahrenheit temperature (°F)	Celsius temperature (°C)	5/9 after subtracting 32